IN 100

FACTS

JEM DUDUCU

Also by the author:
The Busy Person's Guide to British History
The British Empire in 100 Facts
Deus Vult: a Concise History of the Crusades
The Napoleonic Wars in 100 Facts
The Romans in 100 Facts
Forgotten History

You can find me on social media as **@HistoryGems** on Twitter and the same name (with the @) on Facebook and YouTube.

First published 2016

Amberley Publishing
The Hill, Stroud
Gloucestershire, GL5 4EP

www.amberley-books.com

British Library Cataloguing in Publication Data.
A catalogue record for this book is available from the British Library.

ISBN 978 1 4456 5650 2 (paperback)
ISBN 978 1 4456 5651 9 (ebook)

Typeset in 11pt on 13.5pt Sabon.
Typesetting and Origination by Amberley Publishing.
Printed in the UK.

CONTENTS

INTRODUCTION

America was not the first democracy in the world: that would be fifth-century BC Athens. America is not the longest-running democracy: that would be Britain. America is not the largest democracy: that's India. America is, however, the most *important* democracy in the world. Currently, the United States of America is the richest country on Earth and has been for generations – and it's set to be so for at least another one. America's military actions have led to wars in places as far afield as France, the Philippines, Korea and Iraq, to name a few. Its cultural impact is equally vast: who doesn't wear jeans, eat hamburgers and watch blockbuster movies? Britain may have laid the foundations for the modern world, but America wasted no time in building on these foundations.

What is happening in America at any given point in its history is reflected in its democratically elected leader. When America was succumbing to scandal, it had its fair share of scandalous leaders. When America has been strong and resolute so, too, have been its presidents.

It has become fashionable to kick America and all it represents – and let's be clear, it is a flawed country, but aren't all countries flawed? One of the traits of a healthy democracy is that it has the confidence to allow criticism and to have its decisions put under a microscope. As well as America, most Western European countries meet this test; beyond these, many so-called democracies are all too often guilty of suppressing any dissent. America is great not just because of its constitution or its army or its film industry: America is great because it's a land of contrasts and contradictions – and it knows it and can talk freely about it.

This book is a whirlwind tour of 250 years' worth of history. There is no political agenda here, just a chance to cast familiar faces in a new light and to bring forward forgotten presidents (Millard Fillmore anyone?). They all made mistakes because they are human beings and that's what human beings do. But just as there is no political bias, there are no sacred cows here, either.

When doing the research for this book, I found that sources sometimes varied when reporting information one might assume would be a matter of record. Some of the facts regarding early presidents are limited or based on repeated stories – and exactly when certain pieces of key legislation were passed or ratified, approved or enacted is more contentious then you might think. Faced with conflicting information, I tried to go with the most reliable source in the context of the times. To any American political historian who wishes to argue that I got it wrong, I apologise.

Summarising dozens of leaders in the 100 facts format means this book can only provide the briefest of introductions to each of them. The purpose here is to tell a big story as succinctly as possible. I hope you enjoy the journey.

1. You Are Unlikely to Know the Name of the First President of America

Of course most minds will leap to George Washington, but think about that for a moment. During the American Revolutionary War of 1776–1783 (also known as the War of Independence), Washington was a general, not a politician; he was voted in as president in 1789, six years after the end of the War of Independence. So who was doing the governing side of things before Washington?

It is now largely forgotten that, between 1774 and 1788, there were fourteen men who were the 'Presidents' of the Continental Congress. The important difference between these men and Washington (and all other later presidents) is that they were not voted in by the general population but, essentially, by committee.

The first of these was Peyton Randolph of Virginia. Randolph was a lawyer and had served as Attorney General of the Colony of Virginia. However, he resigned from the colonial government in the 1760s as he set about trying to counter (by legal means) the Stamp Act and other unwanted taxation of the American colonies by their British rulers.

Randolph had a keen legal and political mind as well as a proven track record of working against King George's government, so he was a logical choice of candidate for president when delegates from twelve of the thirteen colonies gathered in Philadelphia for the First Continental Congress in 1774. Without much debate he was promptly elected its first president, so we can say that the first American president took office before the Declaration of Independence of 1776 (which was a little presumptuous).

Randolph was instrumental in the creation of the Olive Branch Petition of 1775, which was a final attempt to heal the wounds between the American colonies and the British government before war broke out, but he fell ill and died in that same year. However, the process whereby the Continental Congress elected a president continued for over a dozen more times. Randolph was succeeded by John Hancock of Massachusetts, but like his predecessor he only held office for about a year. None of the leaders were elected by the population at large because there was no federal government infrastructure; they were later fighting a war against the world's largest empire, so everyone was too busy to get out ballot papers.

In effect the president was just another member of the Continental Congress, elected by fellow members to serve as an impartial moderator during its meetings. Designed to be a largely ceremonial position, without much influence, the office was unrelated to the later office of President of the United States. These early presidents did, however, oversee meetings that dealt with nascent foreign policy, the conduct of the Revolutionary War and all the other pressing matters of the time. The last president of the Continental Congress was Cyrus Griffin (another lawyer), who resigned in November 1788 to pave the way for the first general election of a president in 1789. This was won by an ex-British officer by the name of George Washington.

2. George Washington Was the Adopted 'Father' of the Country

It was not always true that you had to be born a US citizen to be president. The first seven presidents were all born before 1776, so they were all British colonists. George Washington, the very first, had strong British credentials.

John Washington was George's great-grandfather and he was born in Purleigh, Essex ... the Essex that's in England. He was an Oxford University don but, in 1657, he set sail as the second officer on a merchant ship to the colony of Virginia. He liked the colony so much that he stayed (and neatly avoided the political turmoil then going on around Oliver Cromwell's republic).

John Washington was a member of a militia group deployed to stop a settlers' rebellion in 1676. The rebellion was stymied but at the expense of a group of Native American chiefs, who were massacred at a planned negotiation. The ex-Oxford don could be brutally practical.

Washington was a tobacco grower in Virginia and depended on slave labour to farm and harvest his crops. His son Lawrence continued the family business, and the Washingtons became part of Virginia's landed gentry, which included his other sons Augustine 'Gus' Washington and George.

The above is really the story of most landed gentry of the age whether they were American, English or French. There's nothing in George's heritage or early career to suggest anything other than aristocratic compliance with the status quo. He even made the most aristocratic of career choices by joining the British Army as a commissioned officer.

The Seven Years' War (1756–1763) is a much sidelined global conflict. It's also horribly complicated. Suffice to say that France, with her Austrian allies, and Britain, with her Prussian allies (led by Frederick the Great), fought a war that would determine exactly which would become the pre-eminent global imperial power. As such, this was a war fought on multiple continents, including North America. Prior to the revolution against Britain, war had already come to the American colonies when both the French and British used Native Americans as proxy forces, which is why the Seven Years' War is referred to in America as the French and Indian War.

Into this maelstrom of war and politics came the young George Washington, who fought his first encounter at the Battle of Jumonville Glen, a battle that raged a full fifteen minutes. Washington lost just one man while the entire French force of forty was either killed or captured. It should be pointed out that Washington was never given an official commission in the British Army and that he fought in the American navy blue, rather than the British red.

Washington proved his effectiveness in a fight, and the Virginian contingent came to be regarded as one of the best and most reliable fighting forces in the colonies. Washington learned much from his experiences in this conflict, but an officer leading colonial forces against the French was about as English an occupation as you could get.

3. WASHINGTON WAS AN AVERAGE GENERAL

As Fact 2 illustrates, Washington never planned to be a rebel leader, let alone become the 'father' of a new nation. After his years of service in the military he settled down to a life typical of the colonial aristocracy. In 1759 he married a wealthy widow, Martha Dandridge Custis, whose lands greatly increased Washington's wealth and social status; and while it was true that he opposed the Stamp Act and became involved with the Continental Congress, he was neither a political leader nor a firebrand revolutionary. In fact, he spent most of this era surveying his lands, playing cards and increasing his holding of slaves. If fate had dealt him a different hand, he would have been a completely forgotten member of the colonial aristocracy.

But the simmering discontent of the colonies, over the not unreasonable request from Britain to pay for some of their costs in the form of taxation, wouldn't go away. The hugely unpopular Stamp Act of 1765 was opposed by Washington and many others, and as events spiralled out of control, Washington declared that it was the colonists' right to stand up against tyranny, or 'custom and use shall make us as tame and abject slaves, as the blacks we rule over with such arbitrary sway'. It's nice to see he recognised how arbitrary American rule over its slave population was.

Revolution turned to war in 1775. Washington was made a full general and given the role of commander-in-chief in the same year, mainly because he turned up to the Congress dressed in his old officer's uniform. He had not been the first leader of American forces in battle, but he had just become the focus of revolutionary conflict with Britain.

Was Washington a great general? The answer is no. He will never stand up against the likes of Alexander the

Great, Julius Caesar, Napoleon or even Frederick the Great. But he was good enough. In 1776 he successfully completed the siege of Boston, but then moved on to New York (which remained loyal to the British Crown throughout the revolution), where he fought the largest battle of the revolution at Long Island – and lost badly. About 20 per cent of his force was killed, wounded or captured. His legendary crossing of the Delaware River and the restructuring of his forces in the brutal cold of Valley Forge were necessary propaganda because he had previously lost too many men in too many battles. It's a myth that most of the revolution involved drably clothed Minutemen ambushing red-jacketed Brits in forests. Most of the battles were conventional affairs, with colonists fighting bravely on both sides.

The reality was that what Britain previously had legally owned in 1774 it now had to fight for, which meant it had lost the argument as soon as the shooting started. Washington hung on long enough (and gained enough French support) to win some late victories and bring Britain to the peace table to talk terms.

4. Washington Finally Became President

After peace was declared and the thirteen colonies became the United States of America, Washington hung up his sword and went back to managing his holdings and playing more cards. However, just as the dust settled on one rebellion over taxes, another flared up. Called Shay's Rebellion, it lasted from 1786 to 1787. It was triggered by the fact that, contrary to popular belief, the colonies were not a better place after independence (it's worth remembering that around 100,000 people left America for Canada, then still a British colony, at the end of the war). The economy was in the doldrums, farmers were finding it hard to turn a profit, land holdings were being foreclosed, and taxation was, once again, a trigger for outrage.

Washington was one of a number of army officers who quickly assembled a militia and put down the rebellion. This was widely seen as the right thing to do and showed that the central government had power and authority. The job done, Washington returned to an easier life and such mundane matters as evicting squatters on some of his holdings.

Against his better judgment, he was pressured into representing Virginia at the Constitutional Convention in 1787, which kept him in the world of politics. In 1789, the Electoral College unanimously elected him as America's first president. This was all before the White House and Capitol Hill existed, so he pledged his oath of office on the balcony of Federal Hall in New York City.

If Washington had been only an average administrator and general, he was a capable and admirable president. Prior to his election, there had been some discussion as to whether America should have a monarch, but the concept did rather fly in the face of the Declaration of Independence. It also seemed a lot of effort to get rid of one King George only to vote in another, so the title 'President' was formalised, and Washington was addressed not as his 'eminence' or his 'excellency', but as 'Mr President'.

It turned out to be a sensible decision not to have a royal title, as in 1789 France was engulfed in the horrors of the French Revolution. As the drums of war sounded out across Europe, Washington wisely declared America to be neutral for the duration of his presidency.

Much of the middle of his time in office dealt with the so-called Whiskey Rebellion, another uprising about taxation (Americans *clearly* hate paying tax). This was finally suppressed in 1794.

In 1796 Washington wrote his farewell address in a letter which touched on all the important political thoughts of the time. It is a remarkable document and a fitting finale for the man who shaped America more than any other. I finish with Washington's own words about unity:

> Every part of our country thus feels an immediate and particular interest in union, all the parts combined cannot fail to find in the united mass of means and efforts greater strength, greater resource, proportionally greater security from external danger.

5. JOHN ADAMS WAS THE FIRST AMERICAN AMBASSADOR TO BRITAIN

John Adams was a more cerebral man than Washington. The first president's background was that of the landed gentry; Adams was a lawyer and, as such, words and ideas were his weapons in the revolution.

Adams was a man of principles, shown most notably by his defence of the British soldiers responsible for the 'Boston Massacre' (when civilians were hurling stones and verbal abuse at British soldiers, they fired into the crowd and five people died). Of the eight accused soldiers, two were found guilty of manslaughter but six were acquitted, so we know Adams was a brilliant lawyer.

Before the outbreak of war Adams had written two books on politics and government and was one of the five men who drafted the Declaration of Independence. During the revolution he went into political overdrive, sitting on ninety committees and chairing twenty-five of them. (And seeing that there were so many of them, it's remarkable the rebels did so well: war by committee is rarely successful.)

Adams recognised that the fight for independence was necessary for his family and future generations of the nascent nation, saying, 'I must study Politics and War that my sons may have the liberty to study Mathematics and Philosophy.'

After the war he was sent to Europe as an ambassador, first to the Netherlands and, later, to Britain as America's first Ambassador to the Court of King George III, a tricky role to say the least. He wasn't exactly welcomed, and when asked about his British ancestry, he retorted, 'You see I have not one drop of blood in my veins but what is American.'

The first contested presidential election occurred in 1796, when John Adams (a Federalist) ran against

Thomas Jefferson (who was seen as a Democratic-Republican). It was an unwieldy system where voters cast votes for two candidates. Although both the votes were for president, the runner-up would become the vice president. The result, in this instance, was the only time in American history when the president and vice president were from different parties. Also, uniquely, Adams kept Washington's entire Cabinet rather than filling it with his own men.

Adams spent the next four years arguing with just about everyone. With hindsight, he was right about most things, at one point steering America away from the brewing hostilities between France and Britain. He also further embedded the concept of 'checks and balances' among the three branches of the US government: the Executive (president), the Judicial (the courts, including the Supreme Court) and the Legislative (Congress). The idea was that no one branch would gain total power, so each would have to compromise, one with the other.

When the next election occurred in 1800, Adams lost narrowly to Jefferson (65 to 73 electoral votes; in American elections, it's the electoral votes that determine the winner). At the time, Adams had only recently moved into the newly completed White House.

Adams' defeat followed shortly after Washington's death in 1799 and led to Federalist disunity (compared to the now better organised Democratic-Republicans).

6. Aaron Burr Was the Most Dangerous American Vice President

Before moving on to Thomas Jefferson, America's third president, it's worth pausing for a look at Aaron Burr, Thomas Jefferson's vice president during his first term of office.

By the time Burr was only two both of his parents had died, and he was raised by his uncle. He was smart and ambitious and was studying law when the American Revolutionary War started. Burr was from the younger generation who, while having been born in the Colonial era, had spent most of their adult lives as Americans. He joined the Continental Army and worked his way up to the rank of lieutenant colonel. He was involved in many engagements, most notably at the Battle of Quebec (which the British won).

While the war ground on, Burr not only fought for independence but also qualified as a lawyer. After the war, he settled in New York. In 1789, his flirtation with politics became serious when he became the New York State Attorney General.

His influence and interest in politics grew over the next fifteen years, and by 1804 Burr had made it to vice president. It was in this role that his relationship with Alexander Hamilton, one of America's Founding Fathers, flared up, and he challenged the first Secretary of the Treasury and the founder of the *New York Post* to a duel. The two men represented the two main political parties of the day: Burr the Democratic-Republicans and Hamilton the Federalists. To add fuel to the fire, Hamilton had been attacking Burr via the press throughout 1804. While there was no love lost between the two men, there was simply too much riding on this personal animosity, and cooler heads should have prevailed. They didn't. Burr shot and mortally wounded Hamilton. Hamilton made it home, where he died the next day. Burr is the only vice president to have killed a man during his term of office ... and he did not go jail.

Unbelievably, this wasn't as controversial as it got for Burr. Next, he was put on trial for treason. Yes, you read that right. Shortly after leaving his role as vice president, Aaron Burr was tried for treason. He was said to be at the head of a conspiracy whose goal was to create an independent country in the centre of North America and parts of present-day Mexico. Burr's version was that he intended to take possession of and farm 40,000 acres (162 km²) in the Texas territory, land that had been leased to him by the Spanish Crown.

Despite no firm evidence, President Thomas Jefferson ordered Burr arrested, and he was indicted for treason. Burr's true intentions remain unclear. Some historians believe he intended to take parts of Texas and some or all of the Louisiana Purchase for himself. Whatever the truth of the matter, Burr was acquitted of the charge, but the trial destroyed his already faltering political career.

War hero, killer and possible traitor: nineteenth-century American politics was far from dull.

7. Thomas Jefferson: Political Thinker, President ... and Real Estate Magnate

Thomas Jefferson was another of the Founding Fathers who was instrumental in the creation of the Declaration of Independence and who was later elected president. Prior to his own presidency, he had been John Adams' vice president, even though they were from different parties.

Jefferson had always been an advocate of republican ideals, and once in office he continued to resist British influence in the Americas. This principle was the backbone of his presidency, but he couldn't entirely escape the politics of the 'old world'. Napoleon was on the rise, and as France had helped America to independence and was battling their mutual enemy of England, relations between the republican-leaning president and the Emperor of France were surprisingly beneficial for both.

The relationship culminated in the 'Louisiana Purchase', misleadingly named because the area of land bought from the French was substantially larger than what later became the state of Louisiana. Indeed, it was this one real estate deal that primed the colonies of the east coast towards becoming a continental power.

These mid-continental lands stretched from the fringes of Canada, through the Dakotas, the whole of Kansas, Missouri and Oklahoma, down to Louisiana, including New Orleans. This tract of land encompassed the entire floodplain of the Mississippi, more than a million square miles of land, purchased at a price of $15 million – less than two cents per acre. This was a ridiculously cheap price even by early nineteenth-century standards.

Quite why Napoleon sold it at such a knockdown price is still a matter of conjecture, but as he had only gained the area a few years earlier from the

Spanish, and as his ongoing wars, while successful, were expensive, it could well have been a case of selling what he couldn't control. Better to dispose of land on another continent than to spend money trying to hold onto it, especially while the fighting in Europe continued.

As always in politics, there was some resistance to Jefferson's acquisition, with a few objectors claiming it to be 'unconstitutional', but in the end he managed to secure Congressional approval. Jefferson understood the need to explore the vast new territory, and he sponsored a number of mapping expeditions to see what they had acquired for their money. The most famous of these was the Lewis and Clark Expedition.

For most of his presidency Jefferson expressed no public views on the issues of slavery or emancipation, but in 1806 he proposed making the international slave trade illegal. Congress passed the bill a year later.

Over the course of his presidency, by restructuring government financial institutions, Jefferson lowered the national debt from $83 million to $57 million. He is regarded as a practical man of immense political foresight, and his legacy meant that the nation was not only substantially bigger, but that its debt obligations were lower as well. All this and not a shot fired in war. Thomas Jefferson, you will be missed.

8. JEFFERSON DID NOT THINK BEING PRESIDENT WAS HIS GREATEST ACHIEVEMENT

In today's world most of our work is specialised. We don't like our politicians to be 'career politicians', but we expect other people to remain in their chosen professions throughout their working lives. You only have to go back a hundred years or so to see that the greatest achievers were polymaths.

Jefferson mastered many disciplines including philosophy, mathematics, horticulture and architecture. He spent forty years erecting, destroying and redesigning the rooms of his Monticello estate. Some of its rooms are octagonal because he found the shape pleasing.

Jefferson was also a voracious reader and collector of books. Back in the early nineteenth century a collection of 100 books would be seen as quite an expansive (and expensive) library. In 1815, Jefferson donated his collection of 6,487 books to the Library of Congress.

Despite his anti-slavery credentials, Jefferson was, like most of the landed gentry of his day, a slave owner. Historians have traditionally portrayed him as a benevolent master, but that legacy has come under scrutiny and remains controversial.

Jefferson was a true overachiever and left instructions that his tombstone should read as follows:

> Here was buried Thomas Jefferson, Author of the Declaration of Independence, of the Statute of Virginia for religious freedom and Father of the University of Virginia.

So Jefferson was certainly proud of his many accomplishments, but the one most conspicuous by its absence is: 'Third President of the United States of America'.

9. JAMES MADISON WAS AMERICA'S FIRST CAREER POLITICIAN

James Madison was America's fourth president, serving from 1809 to 1817, a period some three decades after the Declaration of Independence. While Madison was just about old enough to have served during the revolutionary war, he was only in charge of some local militias and saw no action during the conflict.

However Madison's role as the head of a militia set him up as a public servant and, still in his twenties, he was elected a number of times to the Virginia House of Delegates, which brought him to prominence with one of America's greatest documents, the United States Constitution.

This document is the definitive law of the United States of America. It originally comprised seven articles but has undergone modifications; a total of twenty-seven amendments have been added over the last two centuries. The amendments are broad but important. The First Amendment (in 1791) prohibits Congress (composed of two chambers: the House of Representatives and the Senate) from restricting certain individual freedoms: freedom of religion, freedom of speech, freedom of the press, freedom of assembly and the right to petition (to make a complaint or seek redress without fear of reprisal). The famous Thirteenth Amendment (in 1865) abolished slavery and involuntary servitude. The most recent Twenty-seventh Amendment (in 1992) prevents members of Congress from granting themselves pay rises during the current session.

None of this would have happened without the National Convention of 1787, during which members were encouraged (partly by Madison) to gather and create this document. While Madison was not the final author, he spoke more than two hundred times during the convention to campaign for a robust legal framework for the new nation. It is because of his tireless pursuit of the ideal that Madison has become known as the 'Father of the Constitution'.

Madison's impassioned speeches and his understanding that America was redefining democratic political theory as the country itself evolved meant he was bound to catch the attention of the Founding Fathers, and it was Jefferson who moulded Madison into his protégé. It was in this middle era of his career that he helped found the Democratic-Republican Party when it became apparent that the old Federalist Party was on the wane and that an effective and unified opposition was needed.

It was under Jefferson that Madison became Secretary of State, and as such he was involved in the Louisiana Purchase (Fact 7). However, his greatest contribution (some might say his greatest catastrophe) under the Jefferson presidency was the Embargo Act of 1807. The situation was simple: while France and Britain battled it out, America wanted to remain neutral in order to continue to trade with both sides. Naturally, neither France nor Britain liked this, so the embargo was intended to withhold all US exports from both sides. Apart from the Jefferson administration, nobody liked it. American traders didn't want to lose business, and the British and French wanted to keep trading. The act didn't take the practical realities into account and it was a failure.

10. The War of 1812 Made Madison America's Worst President

What is 'the worst' anything? It's a matter of opinion. With our present-day love of lists on social media and twenty-four-hour news networks filling time with non-news, 'the worst' or, indeed, 'the best' are terms that get overused. And as the list of American presidents grows ever longer, it becomes harder to determine the ultimate highs and lows.

As stated in the previous fact, Madison was instrumental in the creation of the US Constitution. That already gives him some points. However, his attempt to block exports was a failure, and during his term of office he presided over one of America's greatest humiliations, the so-called War of 1812. Madison's adherence to a position of neutrality when acting as Secretary of State seemed to evaporate when he became president.

Throughout the early 1800s, Britain and France were waging endless war to see who would come out on top in the age of empires. While Napoleon seemed largely unstoppable on land, Britain was the same at sea, and maritime warfare affected American trade. This was an unintended consequence, but the effects were real. Similarly, Royal Navy ships 'impressed' (a fancy naval term for kidnapping locals to serve on ships) some Americans. America had every right to feel aggrieved and would have been justified in taking matters to the British government; however, Madison's consequent declaration of war was not only an overreaction but a colossal gamble that failed.

America was then an indebted agrarian nation with a small fleet and a poor peacetime army. It chose to declare war on the world's largest empire, which had an experienced and well-trained army. Perhaps the

Americans calculated that the British were too busy to do much about them, and in a way, they were.

The forces that Britain deployed in America were minuscule compared to their war effort in Europe, but they were enough. British troops headed inland from the coast and from Canada. Detroit fell to the British without a shot fired. The Americans tried to separate Canada from its food sources in the Caribbean, but that failed. Of course, most famously the British successfully captured Washington D.C. and set fire to the White House. While the British didn't plan to stay indefinitely, they remained for weeks, knowing there was no danger of a counter-attack. If a president loses the capital city, he's not a great president.

This war has been misremembered in America as a huge success. It is pointed out that the final battle of the war (in 1815, so the name is already misleading) was a bloody and futile British attempt to capture New Orleans. This is technically correct but fails to take into account that throughout the conflict America was outclassed in every way that counts.

The 1814 peace treaty basically returned everything to the status quo. Quite simply, Britain had bigger fish to fry and a point had been made. But communications in those days were slow and that final battle at New Orleans happened after peace had been declared.

11. THE PRESIDENCY OF JAMES MONROE MARKED THE END OF AN ERA

As the saying goes, 'time and tide wait for no man' and as the years passed, the generation that helped to create America from British colonies was getting older. James Monroe was the fifth president and the last one to have a war record from the War of Independence. His service is quite a story.

The Battle of Trenton in 1776 was fought in late December and, while small, was a much needed morale-boosting victory for the rebels. A well-equipped German mercenary force of Hessians was stationed at Trenton, where it was ensconced in warm quarters recovering from Christmas festivities. Washington led a daring raid on the force, hoping to catch it by surprise, which is exactly what happened. The fighting was fierce but short. The Hessians surrendered and almost two-thirds of the garrison was captured. Most importantly for the rebels, they were able to gain access to much needed food, supplies and new weapons.

Monroe fought in this battle and was seriously wounded when a shot, which lodged in his left shoulder, severed an artery. Monroe was bleeding profusely and, in the freezing conditions of a North American winter, he was not expected to make it; but a doctor was able to staunch the flow of blood, and he recovered, although he fought in no further engagements in the war. For his efforts he was immortalised (inaccurately) as the flag bearer in the painting *Washington Crossing the Delaware*.

12. Monroe Was a Lucky President

While calmer analysis has since prevailed with regard to how bad the War of 1812 was for America, at the time it was seen as a sign that America was now an equal to its old master (it wasn't, but let's not dwell on that). Since the war was popularly seen as a victory and since Monroe had been the Secretary of War towards its end, he enjoyed a strong swell of public support come the election. The opposing Federalist Party had been against the war and didn't even put up a formal candidate in 1812 (although Federalist candidate Rufus King ran against Monroe in 1816, the final presidential candidate of his party before it collapsed). Most politicians would kill to be in this position, but Monroe was simply the right man in the right place at the right time.

The end of the War of 1812 (which, as mentioned previously, actually ended in 1815) introduced what is known in American political history as the 'Era of Good Feelings'. The economy was getting back on its feet, and the war had produced a new national song in 'The Star Spangled Banner'.* The feeling in America was one of unity and pride. Wherever Monroe went, he was greeted by cheering crowds.

Monroe wanted to emulate Jefferson by purchasing land in the Americas owned by European powers. However, when negotiations with Spain over Florida took too long, he sent in the army. This led to outrage not only in Congress but in the imperial governments of Europe, which also protested such a naked land grab. However, Europe was still recovering from twenty-five years of war with France, and nobody was in the mood to slug it out. So although Monroe had overplayed his hand, once again, he was lucky.

Eventually a treaty with Spain was agreed, and the Americans bought Florida for $5 million. The indigenous Seminole tribe was moved off its ancestral lands and relocated to reservations, an appalling practice that would become all too common in nineteenth-century America. In addition, Spain had to give up its lands in the Texas territory. All of this led to the Monroe Doctrine, a declaration by the US government that America had the right to dominate the North American continent and that any act by a European power that sought to interfere would be considered an act of aggression. It was a declaration of imperial expansion, much like Russia was doing in Asia at the time.

Monroe was the president who remembered the revolution and saw the creation of the documents that came to define America. But the Monroe Doctrine was the future. Americans believed it was their destiny to build a nation that stretched from coast-to-coast.

*At the time 'My Country 'Tis of Thee' was a popular national anthem which, rather cheekily, had borrowed the tune of the British national anthem 'God Save the Queen'. 'The Star Spangled Banner' became the official national anthem only in 1931.

13. JOHN QUINCY ADAMS KNEW HOW TO GET WHAT HE WANTED

In Fact 5 John Adams was quoted as saying, 'I must study Politics and War that my sons may have the liberty to study Mathematics and Philosophy.'

It implied that Adams followed a course he hadn't intended but one that had the benefit of giving his children more choice. This is a little ironic as his son, John Quincy Adams, followed in his father's footsteps and was elected America's sixth president a little over a year before his father died.

In his youth Quincy Adams accompanied his father on trips to Europe and became an accomplished linguist. He studied law at Harvard and undertook diplomatic missions before being elected to the Senate in 1802. He was an impressive Secretary of State under President Monroe and helped to formulate the Monroe Doctrine.

Just like his father, the son was an impressive diplomat. He was one of the key American negotiators of the Treaty of Ghent, the peace treaty for the War of 1812. He was also instrumental in the Adams–Onís Treaty, which was the aforementioned purchase of Florida by America from a very angry Spain. In lesser hands both of these treaties with imperial foreign powers could have achieved less for America, so it is to Quincy Adams' credit that, on both occasions, he negotiated good deals for his country.

Adams' political and negotiating skills came to the fore in the presidential election of 1824 in his contest with Andrew Jackson. The election was a mess as both the 'first past the post' and the caucus systems had collapsed. People were voting, but the rules were unclear. That was bad for democracy but good for the extremely shrewd Quincy Adams.

Jackson got more popular votes than Adams, but it was not clear who had won the electoral votes. As confusion reigned, Adams got to work on the House of Representatives. Cutting a long, complex and clearly corrupt story short, John Quincy Adams was elected president even though he had received only a little more than a third of the popular vote. Jackson was furious (it was never a good idea to upset Jackson, but more on that later) and claimed that Adams had made a 'corrupt bargain'. He was right, but it was too late.

Quincy Adams had hustled his way into the White House, but if Jackson wasn't fooled, neither were the voters. The manner in which Adams had secured the presidency hung over his term, and because he had more enemies than friends in Congress he found it hard to pass legislation. He worked to improve the country's communication lines with more and better roads and tackled the national debt (getting it down from $416 million to just $45 million). Recognising that noble causes abroad weren't America's problem, he avoided foreign entanglements. Adams wanted to do more but couldn't garner the support; he also wanted a second term of office, but Jackson won emphatically in 1829.

John Quincy Adams is an example of 'be careful what you wish for, lest it come true'.

14. John Quincy Adams Was a Colourful Character

One of the issues with formal portraits and the fashion of times gone by is that people always look somewhat stern. When you add the veneer of power that comes with being president, it's easy to assume that these people spent all their time being serious, doing noble deeds and/or scheming for more power.

It's important to remember that all of the presidents had personalities of their own, and all of them had personal interests. However, John Quincy Adams stands out from this crowd as having done some pretty unusual things. For example, he got up every morning at 5.00 a.m. to swim the Potomac River naked. This became so well known that a female reporter, Ann Royall, stole his clothes and sat on them, refusing to hand them over until he agreed to give her an interview, thus becoming the first woman to interview an American president (though, presumably, not just as he emerged from the river).

He charged the government $61 for a pool table at the White House, which was so mocked as a sign of his aristocratic tastes that he had to reimburse the treasury. He also kept a 'pet' alligator in a bath in the East Wing of the White House and enjoyed scaring guests when showing them around. You could say he had a pretty snappy sense of humour (apologies).

As strange as all this sounds, there is a stranger story associated with Quincy Adams. In 1818 an American officer called Captain John Cleves Symmes, Jr. published his *Circular No. 1*, which opened with the line:

> To the World! I declare the earth is hollow, and habitable within …

It's never a good sign when a new scientific theory starts with a sentence that ends in an exclamation mark. Symmes published more articles and went on speaking tours, building on his original model to later include 'mole people' who inhabited the interior of the Earth.

Unbelievably (but true) John Quincy Adams became excited about the idea and put together the funding for an expedition to the Arctic Circle, where it was proposed that they drill a hole that would take them to the Earth's interior and they would meet these mole people. So the next time you think that the government is being wasteful of taxpayers' money, remember that at least they aren't paying for expeditions to meet imaginary beings.

Thankfully, for the sake of the taxpayers, Quincy Adams' reputation and the explorers who would have met their icy deaths, the expedition didn't happen. Quincy Adams failed to get re-elected, and Andrew Jackson, the seventh president, was not the kind of man to be taken in by such fanciful ideas.

While all of this is amusing, it should be pointed out that Quincy Adams was one of the presidents most staunchly opposed to slavery (many of the previous presidents had owned slaves and Monroe even brought some to the White House). He fought tirelessly to end the scourge.

15. A House Painter Called Richard Lawrence Made History

Richard Lawrence was a house painter who had immigrated to America with his family at the turn of the nineteenth century. He was, in many ways, an average person, but as he got older he became more and more erratic. At one point he told his family he was going back to England, only to return a month later, declaring he had changed his mind because it was too cold. Unfortunately he became obsessed with Andrew 'Old Hickory' Jackson, who finally became president in 1829.

The two men's worlds notably intersected at a funeral in January of 1835. Lawrence had been following Jackson for some time and was seen to be agitated on the day. As he left a paint shop, he was heard to mutter to himself, 'I'll be damned if I don't do it.'

When Jackson was walking away from the funeral gathering, Lawrence stepped out behind the president, raised and fired a pistol. Nothing happened. However Lawrence had been thorough in his plans and raised a second pistol, but this, too, failed to fire. Jackson was a man of action in every possible sense, and on this occasion he showed Lawrence just why he was sometimes called 'Old Hickory' as he wielded his hickory walking stick and beat senseless his would-be assassin. Jackson was in his late sixties but still had enough fire in his belly to retaliate against the man who had tried to kill him. This was the first assassination attempt carried out against a sitting President of the United States of America.

In the ensuing court case, Lawrence explained that he associated the president with the loss of his job, and that by killing Jackson he hoped for a better world. He also informed the court that he was not just Richard Lawrence but Richard III, King of England (who had been dead for some 350 years). Because of such outlandish statements and other testimony about his ever more bizarre behaviour, he was found 'not guilty by reason of insanity' and institutionalised for the rest of his life.

As crazy as Lawrence was, his plot didn't fail because he was stupid. When the two pistols were inspected, they were found to be new and in good working order. However, later research suggested that this particular model was prone to misfire in damp conditions, which would have been the case on that late January day in Washington D.C.

Many more attempts would be made on other presidents' lives – some successful, some not. Like these later attempts, conspiracy theories were linked to Lawrence's action, but there was never any evidence to implicate anyone else in this assassination attempt.

Putting science to one side, the president had been saved by two misfires from pistols. It felt as if Providence had had a hand. The same divine blessing that had nurtured this young nation through good times and bad had intervened once again and convinced the country that Jackson was the embodiment of everything American.

16. Andrew Jackson Was (Possibly) Guilty of Crimes against Humanity

For most of American presidential history, the president tended to be either a great thinker or orator, such as Jefferson, Adams and, later, Lincoln, or a man of action, known for his bravery in war, like Washington, Jackson and, later, Grant. Andrew Jackson was not an officer during the American Revolutionary War (he was too young to serve although he did pass messages for the rebels), but he was the hero of the War of 1812, mounting the defence and winning eventual victory against the British at New Orleans.

That war wasn't Jackson's earliest lethal encounter. In 1806 Charles Dickinson (who competed with Jackson in horse-breeding circles) remarked in a local newspaper that Jackson was 'a worthless scoundrel, a poltroon and a coward' and, for good measure, insulted Mrs Jackson's honour. A Carolina man can take only so much besmirching of his good name, and Jackson challenged Dickinson to a duel. Dickinson fired first, hitting Jackson in the chest; Jackson fired second and mortally wounded Dickinson. No charges were brought against the future president, and Jackson carried the bullet in his chest for the rest of his days.

Jackson didn't do 'subtle'. It was under his presidency that there was an escalation in the resettlement of Native Americans, which led to the period known in that community as the 'Trail of Tears'. 'Resettlement' sounds like the process was well organised, but it wasn't. As entire tribes were pushed further west, tens of thousands died from exposure, hypothermia, starvation and disease. It's worth pointing out that similar events happened to the Armenians under Ottoman rule in the early twentieth century, and there have been mounting calls to describe these death marches as 'genocide'.

If that's the term that should be used to describe what happened to the Armenians, then Andrew Jackson and the American government are also guilty of genocide in respect of Native Americans. The land may have been part of the Louisiana Purchase, but the Cherokee and Chickasaw tribes were unaware that their ancestral homes were property of the French and had been sold to a new landlord.

Not all tribes went peacefully. Jackson made more than seventy treaties with local tribes, and while some resigned themselves to their fate, others fought. It was during Jackson's presidency that the Second Seminole War erupted in Florida. Lasting more than six-and-half years, some 9,000 US troops were sent to Florida to hunt down fewer than 1,000 Native American warriors. By the end of the war, the US Army had suffered more than 1,500 casualties. While some of the Seminole tribe did relocate, the rest stayed behind, and the situation led to a third war a little over a decade later.

Jackson was a man of his time. Brave and honourable in the framework of his own society, he waged expansionist wars with no regard for indigenous peoples. In this respect America was acting just like the European powers of the time.

17. ANDREW JACKSON AVOIDED TWO WARS

Andrew Jackson was a man of contradictions. While overseeing the forced resettlement of Native Americans, he adopted two native children. Similarly with slavery, he was sensitive to both sides of the issue. By the 1830s, more and more European countries were abolishing slavery, but most of the economies of the southern states were dependent on slave plantations. The problem was how to abolish slavery without plunging the South into an economic depression. (This is clearly an economic viewpoint and not a moral one; the 'right' thing to do was to abolish slavery).

One bone of contention was that northerners were sending anti-slavery tracts throughout the US by means of the postal system. Such propaganda was seen as outrageous in the South, which wanted to ban them from being sent via the US Mail. Jackson sought a compromise, doing his best to stitch together two sides separated by a gulf of opinion. A skilful negotiator, he avoided splits and war, something that would happen later in the century.

But oppression at the time was felt not just by black slaves. Settlers in Texas believed they owed no allegiance to the Mexican government and wanted independence. It was during Jackson's presidency that Texas broke away from Mexico (with the famous last stand at the Alamo becoming a hallowed moment in American history). Jackson shrewdly recognised the Republic of Texas, a move that could have provoked war with Mexico. But the anticipated war did not happen, and, eventually, the republic became an American state.

18. MARTIN VAN BUREN COULD HAVE COINED THE PHRASE 'IT'S THE ECONOMY STUPID'

That quote is from the much later President Bill Clinton's election campaign, but Van Buren's one-term presidency was defined solely by a recession that crippled the nation in the late 1830s.

As his name suggests, Van Buren came from a Dutch family, and Dutch was the language spoken in his home. He studied law and was admitted to the bar in 1803. However, even before he qualified he had been involved in politics. Much like Madison, Van Buren was a career politician. While Jackson was fighting in the War of 1812, Van Buren was working in the New York State Senate, enlarging the state's militia and getting the soldiers better pay. This was important work but not exactly the stuff of legend.

The above is, in essence, the problem with Van Buren. What he did was significant and necessary, but it's all rather dry. In 1821 he became a US Senator for New York and proceeded to debate tariffs to improve roads and bridges. Logistics and transportation are vital, but the subjects are seldom captivating. However, by understanding the government machine, he eventually became Jackson's vice president and, thanks largely to Jackson's backing (and his immense popularity), Van Buren soon thereafter became the eighth president in 1837 ... at exactly the moment the wheels fell off the economy.

While Britain had no direct power over America, it still had substantial indirect power through the banks of the British Empire. America's expansion in the 1820s and 30s was on the back of loans secured through various British banks – banks which started to raise interest rates in 1837, sending prices (and the cost of debt) spiralling upwards in America. There was no plot. The British banks were worried about cash flow, and the rate increases were within the norms of the time, but the moves had a disproportionate impact on the American economy. The resulting depression lasted for more than five years. Unemployment peaked, as did inflation, while profits and wages slumped.

The depression affected everyone from the farmers of the South to the merchants on the East Coast. The American banking system was shattered: of the 850 banks in America at that time, 343 closed and 62 suffered partial failures. Hundreds of millions of dollars were lost – and that figure is not adjusted for inflation.

None of this was Van Buren's fault, but as he had been in the government for so long it was hard to disassociate him from the economic mess now that he was president. He went from winning his first term by a landslide to facing a furious public as he sought a second term. The opposition Whig Party declared him to be 'Martin Van Ruin', a nickname that dogged him throughout the campaign. It came as no surprise that Whig candidate William Harrison won nineteen states to Van Buren's seven.

Van Buren attempted to become a presidential candidate again in both 1844 and 1848, but he never returned to the centre stage in politics.

19. Martin Van Buren Was the First American-Born President

While Van Buren's presidency is really only of interest to the most academic of presidential historians, there are some interesting facts about his life.

As the title states, Van Buren was the first president born after the Declaration of Independence. He was born in Kinderhook, New York in 1782. Kinderhook is important because it was the basis of his nickname 'Old Kinderhook', which during his first presidential election was abbreviated to 'OK' and is thought to be where the term 'OK' (okay) comes from. (This is contested by some Scottish historians who think it comes from the Scottish slang for 'oh yes', which sounds like 'och aye'.)

While Van Buren's presidency was one of economic failure, earlier in his career he was involved in a romantic scandal, which came to be known as the 'Petticoat Affair'. While in Jackson's Cabinet, John Eaton (the Secretary of War) courted a widower of low social status. It was believed that Eaton and the new Mrs Eaton may have had a relationship before her first husband died. This caused a scandal, and so Van Buren resigned, allowing Jackson to dismiss the rest of his Cabinet. This was all very Victorian in its political outlook. Imagine if, in today's world, a misbehaving Cabinet member was caught in a scandal. No one would expect the entire Cabinet to be cleared out over the shocking revelations of one.

Van Buren's lengthy autobiography has two strange omissions: his wife is never mentioned ... nor is his presidency.

20. William Henry Harrison Made History for All the Wrong Reasons

William Henry Harrison was sixty-eight when he won a landslide victory and became America's ninth president. His presidency capped an illustrious political and military career, and he was set to guide America out of economic recession. That's probably what Harrison intended and what he hoped his legacy would be, but that's not what happened.

Harrison had previously run for president in 1836, but against the Jackson-backed juggernaut that saw the election of the then Vice President Van Buren, Harrison stood little chance and returned to his farm in Ohio after an inevitable defeat.

His comfortable election win in 1840 hinged on him being a war hero and a salt-of-the-earth man you could trust. After all, he was a farmer and farmers don't make sneaky politicians … apparently. At his inauguration Harrison wanted to capitalise on his reputation for bravery while also dispelling the opposition's caricature of him as a backward farmer, so he made some unfortunate decisions.

4 March 1841 was an unusually cold, wet day for the time of year, but the new president arrived at his swearing-in ceremony not in a carriage (too aristocratic), but on horseback. To make matters worse, he wore no overcoat or hat. While he wanted everyone to be able to have a good look at their new president, he was obviously feeling the cold. Worse still, in what was appalling weather, he chose to make the longest inaugural address in American history. His speech took nearly two hours to read, which proved only that he lacked basic common sense.

To add further stress to his ageing body, after the address he slowly rode on horseback through the streets of the capital to acknowledge the cheering crowds. It was still cold and wet. And just when most people might have wanted to put their feet up, he changed out of his wet clothes and went on to attend three inaugural balls that evening.

Three weeks later, Harrison came down with pneumonia. While this can be seen as too long a gap to say that he became ill as a result of his inaugural day exposure to the elements, no doubt the events of that day would have weakened him, making him vulnerable to infections.

Doctors tried a number of medical treatments in their attempts to cure Harrison, but they all failed. He lapsed into delirium and died on 4 April. Modern doctors think it was enteric fever which finally finished him off.

Harrison's presidency set a number of records. After just thirty-two days in office, it was, unsurprisingly, the shortest presidency in history. He was the last president born a British subject (i.e. before 1776), and he was also the oldest president to be elected (until Ronald Reagan, more than a century later). He was also the first president to die in office. So, there are quite a few records linked to the man, but it's safe to say that he would have wanted almost none of them next to his name.

21. John Tyler Was an Accidental President

According to the US Constitution, Article II, Section 1, Clause 5:

> In Case of the Removal of the President from Office, or of his Death, Resignation, or Inability to discharge the Powers and Duties of the said Office, the same shall devolve on the Vice President.

It sounds officious, but is vague when it comes to the question of who, exactly, would be the new president following the sudden death of Harrison. In the hours just afterwards, the Cabinet met to discuss what the Constitution intended and came to the conclusion that the current vice president, John Tyler, was 'Vice President Acting President'.

When Tyler arrived in the capital a short time later, he was confident that he was not only 'acting president' but that he was, in fact, the legitimate tenth President of the United States. He wasted no time having himself immediately sworn in (in his hotel room), without any qualifiers. Harrison's Cabinet seemed to accept this resolution, but his political opponents never recognised him as president. He was openly mocked with snide nicknames, one being 'His Accidency'.

The opposition Whig Party went on to cause as much trouble as they could for Tyler. Just a few months into his presidency, the federal government faced a projected budget deficit of $11 million. The proposed solution was to increase tariffs. However, while this made fiscal sense, in the midst of an economic downturn, it was an immensely unpopular move. The majority Whig Congress fought against it and eventually threw it out.

Tyler was forced to use his presidential veto, which ensured he made more political enemies.

After lurching from crisis to crisis, things actually got worse for Tyler. In July of 1842 he became the first president to have impeachment proceedings brought against him. John Quincy Adams headed a House Select Committee which attacked and condemned Tyler's use of his veto. The committee's report did not go as far as recommending impeachment proceedings, but it established the possibility as a point of law. The committee's conclusions were endorsed by a vote of 98–90 in favour of the findings. Tyler was becoming ever more isolated.

While Tyler was reeling from internal difficulties, he did better in international affairs. In 1842 he began the process that would annex Hawaii. Seeing that the islands had been of interest to Britain and were 2,471 miles away from the west coast of the North American continent, this was no mean feat. In 1845, just three days before leaving office, Tyler officially annexed the Republic of Texas into the Union. Neither Texas nor Hawaii was yet an American state but the process started with Tyler.

Tyler was an unusual president. Over the course of his career he switched parties on several occasions, which meant that by the time of the election of 1844 he had run out of allies and wasn't selected by either the Whigs or the Democrats as a candidate. That election was contested between James K. Polk and Henry Clay – with Polk becoming president.

22. Emergency Presidential Succession Was Created by Tyler

When Harrison died in office, there was a flurry of legal discussions about what exactly the US Constitution meant regarding the role and powers of a vice president in the event of the death of the president. The Cabinet had come up with a different reading of the situation than had Tyler but acquiesced to Tyler's decisive action (probably because he retained Harrison's Cabinet in its entirety). In every way that mattered, Tyler had become president and, in so doing, set the precedent for all future scenarios involving the death or impeachment of the president.

This was a pivotal moment in American history. When Lincoln and Kennedy were assassinated, when Roosevelt died of natural causes and when Nixon resigned, Tyler's precedent that the vice president would seamlessly slot into the presidential seat was used to ensure the smooth transition of power. Andrew Johnson, Lyndon Johnson, Harry Truman and Gerald Ford were all vice presidents who had no reason to suspect that they would lead their country without ever having been voted in as president. More on these men later, but it's interesting that a few, like Tyler, couldn't get past the fact that they were, in essence, walking in dead men's shoes. Two would subsequently be voted in for a further term in office.

All of these incongruities can be traced back to Tyler who, because of the short duration of Harrison's presidency, holds the dubious record of serving longer than any president who was never elected to the office.

23. There Was a Dark Horse President

James Polk was born in North Carolina, the eldest of ten in a family of Scots-Irish parentage. In his late teens he suffered from severe abdominal pains, which required surgery at a time when the only anaesthetic was strong liquor. Although the surgery to remove kidney stones was successful, it was thought that this operation made him sterile as he never had any children.

Polk's formal education didn't start until he was eighteen when the family moved to Tennessee. He was obviously a quick learner as, just three years later, he was accepted at the University of North Carolina. He graduated with Honours (I'm British, the publisher is British, so we're using British spellings) in 1818 and studied law under a well-known Nashville trial attorney, Felix Grundy. A year later, and with Grundy's endorsement, Polk was elected clerk for the Tennessee State Senate. He was admitted to the bar and set up his own legal practice a year after that. This was an amazing change in fortunes. In just six years Polk had gone from having no formal education, had graduated from university and was now working in the state senate. A year on from that, he was a qualified lawyer with his own successful practice. It seems fair to conclude that Polk was a man of tenacity and intellect, a man who should not be underestimated.

In 1822 Polk joined the Tennessee militia as a captain in the cavalry, and in the same year resigned his position as clerk to run his campaign for the Tennessee State Legislature. He won. A year later and he became the new representative of Maury County, Tennessee – the same year that Polk voted for Andrew Jackson to become the next US Senator from Tennessee, a link with Jackson that would see Polk follow in his footsteps.

In 1824 Polk married Sarah Childress, who had attended the Salem Female Academy in North Carolina and would become the best educated First Lady up until that time. She later helped Polk write speeches and deal with official presidential correspondence.

In 1825 Polk won a seat in the US House of Representatives. Every year since leaving university he was making political progress. Fast forwarding ten years to 1835, he was now Speaker of the House. In 1838 he left the House of Representatives and, a year later, became Governor of Tennessee.

When it came to the presidential election of 1844, there were numerous nominees, all jostling for positions within their parties. Polk was not expected to be the Democratic nominee, and for the first time in American political history the term 'dark horse', meaning an outsider of unknown ability, was used in reference to Polk's chances against the Whig candidate, Henry Clay. While Polk received only 50 per cent of the popular vote (a vital 2 per cent went to James Birney), he won 170 of the electoral votes to Clay's 105, and James K. Polk became the eleventh President of the United States.

24. James K. Polk's Borders Knew No Limits

James Polk, while not unique, was certainly impressive in that he resolved all the issues he had highlighted in his election campaign. The next time someone says, 'All politicians are liars', you can reply, 'But what about James Polk?' (I'm pretty sure the response will be 'who?', but you get my point.)

One of the key issues of the time was the continuation of America's belief in its 'manifest destiny' that all of continental America, from coast to coast, would one day be encompassed in the contiguous United States of America. The areas that Polk focussed on were the Oregon Country plus California and New Mexico.

Oregon was part of an ongoing border dispute with British-held Canada. Initially, Polk wanted the 54°40' parallel to be the border. This led to the bizarrely specific chant 'fifty-four forty or fight!' at some of his rallies during the election of 1844. Although a little further south than he had originally wanted, Polk agreed a peaceful and ratified border with Canada. The positioning of the Canadian–American border at the 49th parallel had the immediate effect of formalising areas into American lands that would eventually become the states of Oregon, Idaho and Washington. It also created what would become the longest peaceful border in the world.

Meanwhile, further south, when President Tyler annexed Texas it was Polk who was waiting in the wings, and it was done with his blessing. But Mexico believed it owned the land and shots were fired. Polk offered to buy the disputed territory, but the Mexicans refused, and the resulting conflict led to the Mexican–American War (1846–1848). American forces were incredibly efficient and scored their easiest victory against a foreign nation so far in their history. They quickly occupied the disputed lands, and from there invaded northern Mexico proper. The Pacific Squadron took control of several garrisons on the Pacific coast in Baja California. Finally, General Winfield Scott captured the capital, Mexico City.

This overwhelming victory forced the Mexican government, led by Santa Anna (the same man who won at the Alamo), to the negotiating table; and in 1848, the Treaty of Guadalupe Hidalgo was signed. Various fines were paid and populations were allowed to move to whichever country they wished. However, the most important sections of the treaty required Mexico's recognition of the annexation of Texas, and gave the US ownership not only of California but also a large area comprising roughly half of New Mexico, most of Arizona, Nevada, Utah and parts of Wyoming and Colorado (as they were to become).

In a brief period and at relatively little cost in terms of money spent or loss of life, Polk significantly increased the lands under American control. In 1848 he even offered to buy Cuba from Spain, but Spain declined.

Polk only wanted to serve for one term and, much as he had done throughout his life, left office having made substantial achievements in a short space of time. He died just a few months later in 1849, aged fifty-three.

25. THE ELECTION OF 1848 WAS AN HISTORIC ONE

When James Polk decided not to seek a second term as president, the election of 1848 became an open race. It should be noted that there is always a discrepancy between the time a president is elected and when he takes office. Elections always take place in even years (today, in 2016, in November), and the incumbent president always takes office the following year (currently in January). The reason for the delay is due to the problems of communication in early America. Before the telegraph, let alone the telephone, it took weeks to spread the news of an election result. While this made everything fair in the nineteenth century, in the digital world 'tradition' is the only explanation for the interim that still exists.

The election of 1848 is an interesting one because it was the first one to include Texas. It also had three candidates. This was not a unique situation (the 1844 election also had three candidates), but in this instance the third candidate did not represent either of the two main parties. The candidates were Zachary Taylor of the Whig Party, Lewis Cass of the Democratic Party and Martin Van Buren of the Free Soil Party (well done, Martin, for finding a party name worse than 'Whig'). So while the two main parties had candidates who had never been president, they were both up against a man who had held the office. The Free Soil Party may have had a terrible name, but it backed a noble cause: its sole purpose was to prevent the spread of slavery into new territories.

The choice the candidates represented was, in a way, a microcosm of US presidential history. Zachary Taylor (Whig) was the grizzled military veteran of a number of wars. Lewis Cass (Democratic Party) was the career politician (and a Freemason as so many of the early political leaders were), while Martin Van Buren, as a former president, could be judged by his term in office.

The results were not as might be expected. In its first election, Texas voted Democratic and picked the career politician from New Hampshire over the military man from Virginia. However, Taylor and the Whigs carried the day overall by winning both a popular majority and the majority of electoral votes (Taylor's 163 to Cass's 127).

So what of Martin Van Buren and the Free Soilers? They received just over 10 per cent of the national vote, an emphatic rejection of both the former president and a new third party. In a way this wasn't unexpected. While the North was increasingly anti-slavery and the South was entrenched, everyone was doing their best to tiptoe around the subject. At the time the Free Soil Party was too obvious in its message, and even in the 1840s it was recognised that tackling the abolition of slavery might well lead to a constitutional crisis. The issue had been sidestepped for the moment, and in 1849 Zachary Taylor was sworn in as the twelfth president.

26. A NUMBER OF FUTURE PRESIDENTS SERVED IN THE 1832 BLACK HAWK WAR

When Major General Zachary Taylor was elected in 1848 he was the highest ranking officer to become president since George Washington. He had served in the army for over forty years and fought in four separate wars against three very different types of enemy.

Taylor's military career started in 1808, and he first saw action as a young captain in the War of 1812. His first enemy was the conventional army of the British Empire. Although not the most important, it was his second war that is probably the most interesting. In the summer of 1832, a Native American chieftain called Black Hawk brought a mixture of tribes known as the 'British Band' into the Illinois territories. The area had once been Native American land but was now under US government control, and as the return had not been sanctioned it came as a surprise to the authorities. (At the time, the US government regarded the Native Americans as savages, squatting on land that needed to be civilised).

Whether Black Hawk was looking for a fight is a contested point, but his move was an obvious provocation to white settlers in the region. The man in charge of the US response force was General Henry Atkinson, who led a small army composed of a core of regular troops, a large band of militia and hundreds of Native American allies.

Between the months of May and August of 1832, there were a number of battles (in reality, most 'battles' of this period, known as the 'Indian Wars', would be, by European standards, more accurately described as skirmishes, with hundreds, rather than thousands involved). The Native Americans were worn down by hunger and desertion, and Black Hawk's forces were annihilated: a victory for the US government. Although Black Hawk himself managed to evade capture, he later handed himself in. The attempted resettlement of the land by Native Americans was permanently stopped, and the war strengthened the government's resolve to push indigenous tribes west of the Mississippi River.

What makes this minor episode of American history interesting in the context of this book is who was serving in Atkinson's officer corps at the time. Zachary Taylor was, by then, a colonel. However, most intriguingly, both Abraham Lincoln and Jefferson Davis, the leaders on opposite sides of the later American Civil War, were fighting on the same side.

This was not Zachary Taylor's last war for he would go on to be one of the leaders in the earlier mentioned Second Seminole War in Florida. However it was his leadership in the emphatic American victory in the Mexican–American War that brought him fame. That conflict had just ended in 1848, and Taylor campaigned as the mastermind of America's greatest military victory. The news was still fresh in everyone's minds.

Even though he had served effectively in a war started by the Democratic President James Polk, and even though his personal politics were hazy, Taylor had run and won as the Whig candidate.

27. Zachary Taylor Was Meant to Solve the Problem of Slavery

Looking at Facts 25 & 26, you can see that slavery was becoming such a hot topic that those, like Van Buren, who were talking about ending it were seen as too controversial. Because Taylor was so removed and vague on the subject, he had been seen as eminently electable.

In fact, Taylor was such an old warhorse, with such mild views on politics, that there was serious debate in the Whig Party about whether he should be their candidate. While Taylor himself was a slave owner, he did not believe the practice should spread into the newly acquired territories, a colossal stretch of the continental United States from Washington state, through Montana up to and including Minnesota, to the areas that are now California and Nevada – basically everywhere from the central United States westwards (apart from Texas). This is more than half of modern-day America.

There were multiple issues, enough for a lengthy academic book, so let's summarise by saying that America was in several administrative binds: It had an enormous area of land it now owned but did not govern. Gold had been discovered in California; was this US government land? Texas, because of its past as a Mexican territory, claimed ownership of New Mexico, but surely a state couldn't own a territory that would eventually become another state ... could it? However, most importantly, if slaves escaped from a southern state, it was unclear whether recapturing them in these territories was legal or not. It was also unclear if you could own slaves in the new lands. While the term 'Wild West' was applied to these areas only later in the century, in a way it was here that the 'Wild West' began. Laws were vague; the territories were a lawless frontier.

Congress started to work on a series of bills which would become known as the Compromise of 1850, but for more than half a century the fate of slavery hung in the balance. For a soldier like Taylor, who, despite his position as president, had little interest in politics, it was a striking piece of political compromise, and it's unclear if, given the chance, he would have vetoed it. Taylor pushed for California to become a state even before the bill was signed, which ensured it would not be an area that allowed slavery. This shocked the South as it had seen Taylor as 'one of us'; however, Taylor's prime motivation was not about slavery but about preserving the Union. The final bill fudged a number of the issues, but it was viewed as a reasonable compromise simply because neither side could claim victory or defeat.

Taylor never saw the passage of the final bill. Less than two years into his presidency, he died of a stomach-related illness in July of 1850 (the suggestion that he was poisoned by pro-slavery conspirators is completely unfounded). After the straightforward work of soldering, he didn't enjoy politics, saying on his death bed, 'My motives have been misconstrued, and my feelings most grossly outraged.'

28. Millard Fillmore Was the Last Whig President

Thanks to John Tyler's grab for the office of president after the death of Harrison, the demise of Zachary Taylor didn't trigger a constitutional crisis. There was now a precedent for what happened next. Taylor's vice president was Millard Fillmore and so, thanks to Tyler, Fillmore seamlessly filled Taylor's shoes to become the thirteenth president.

Even though both Zachary Taylor and Millard Fillmore had run as Whig candidates, they were in most respects polar opposites. The veteran army officer from the South was replaced by a northern lawyer, career politician and the founder of the University of Buffalo. They can't have had much to talk about. Indeed, recognising that there would be a change in priorities, Taylor's entire Cabinet offered their resignations, which Fillmore accepted.

Fillmore supported the Compromise of 1850, and under his leadership it was signed into law. While it did not resolve the simmering resentments between slave-holding states and free states, it put the genie back in the bottle for a time. This allowed Fillmore to look beyond America's borders. The country was increasingly interested in the Pacific as a sphere of influence. Now that Hawaii had been recognised as an American territory (even though there was still a King of Hawaii, reminding us that America may have been seen as a country, but it was, in fact, an empire – one in the Roman mould that was exceptional at absorbing locals into the nation) America cast its eyes further east, and, in 1852, Fillmore ordered Commodore Matthew C. Perry to try and open up Japan.

The nation of Japan had been closed off from the outside world since the early 1600s. Fillmore's scheme was, in a way, almost as ludicrous as John Quincy Adams sanctioning an expedition to the centre of the Earth. Unbelievable as it was, Commodore Perry succeeded in making contact with the Japanese: his was the first Western interaction with the country for centuries. Because of the time it took for the expedition, Perry did not to return to America until after Fillmore's term of office.

While the Compromise of 1850 saved the Union for a time, it was the beginning of the end of the Whig Party. The party split along pro-slavery and anti-slavery lines, which meant it was no longer an effective opposition to the Democratic Party. The Whigs were subsumed into the Republican Party and the anti-immigration American Party (even though all of its members were white descendants of immigrants). This party was also known as the 'Know Nothings' because when it was first established it was semi-secret, so members, when asked about it, would reply, 'I know nothing.'

Millard Fillmore did everything that could reasonably be expected of a president. He held the country together and expanded its influence, but he couldn't know that his actions would be directly linked to the demise of his party. The signs were there at the 1852 Whig National Convention when he wasn't even selected as the Whig presidential candidate in that year's election.

29. Millard Fillmore's Life Was a 'Rags to ... Obscurity' Story

Much has been made of the fact that Abraham Lincoln was born in a log cabin and came from poor country stock, eventually overcoming his deprived background to rise to the highest office in the land (the ultimate tale of the American Dream). Exactly the same can be said of Millard Fillmore. His parents were dirt poor and, like Lincoln's, eager to see their children rise above poverty. As a young man Fillmore worked as an apprentice cloth maker and from that point began to study law.

It is here, however, that any comparison to Abraham Lincoln ends. Lincoln is, arguably, the greatest president in American history, whereas Fillmore, the last Whig president and a president who achieved little, is seen, in part, as the end of an era. The opening up of Japan is exotic but not of great significance in American history. Similarly, the 1850 Compromise, while well meaning, did not stop the country's slide into civil war.

On the plus side, we can say that Fillmore was personally brave because, in December of 1851, he helped to put out a fire at the Library of Congress and later raised a bill for funds to restock the library.

While it is true that he dragged himself up by the bootstraps, he certainly had a chip on his shoulder. His first elected office was to the New York State Assembly where, in 1828, he was elected on an anti-Masonic ticket. The Freemasons (Masons) were America's privileged elite, but it seems he resented not being one of them.

Fillmore was unpopular with northern Whigs because he had signed the Fugitive Slave Act (which allowed the return of captured slaves in US territory), part of the 1850 Compromise. This, in large part, deprived him of the Whig nomination in 1852, after which he returned to his law practice in Buffalo. However, his political ambitions were not over, and four years later he was back, representing the American 'Know Nothing' Party. Now he was not just anti-Masonic, he was also anti-Catholic and anti-immigrant. It all seemed like sour grapes.

Briefly leapfrogging the 1852 election, the election of 1856 was one for the history books. It was the first time that the Republican Party put forward a candidate, and it was also another three-party race. The hopeless Free Soil Party had all but given up, so the third party on this occasion was Fillmore's; and for the first time in American electoral history, it carried one state – Maryland – but that was it. Fillmore managed only 22 per cent of the popular vote. This wasn't helped when, after announcing his candidacy, he 'campaigned' by leaving the country for months.

Later, during the Civil War, Fillmore denounced the secession of the South while also criticising the war policies of President Abraham Lincoln. As a consequence he was ignored by both North and South. He died of a stroke in 1874. His last words were something about some soup. Is it any wonder that the White House's official website calls him 'uninspiring'?

30. Franklin Pierce Was Always up for a Fight

After the well-meaning but inauspicious presidency of Millard Fillmore, the nation was ready to go in a different direction, and it chose the Democrat Franklin Pierce of New Hampshire in the 1852 election. Most of Pierce's early politics were what might be expected from a northern Democrat, but another side of the man was yet to emerge. Pierce was an established lawyer and had achieved the position of United States Attorney for New Hampshire under James Polk's presidency. When war with Mexico broke out, he put aside his political career and donned a colonel's uniform. He was later promoted to brigadier-general under General Winfield Scott.

In his first engagement at the Battle of Contreras, his horse tripped and fell on him, pinning him to the ground and badly injuring his knee, making it virtually impossible for him to ride. When he was ordered to the rear during a later battle, he pleaded with the general to be allowed to fight and led his troops tied to his saddle; his leg was so painful he passed out and was moved behind the front lines. This is most unusual behaviour for a United States Attorney. Whether it was because he thought a military record would help his political career or whether he was just always itching for a fight, we will never know.

While some saw his fainting and falling in two battles as a sign of cowardice, others saw him as a fighter. He certainly fought tenaciously to become the Democratic presidential candidate in the 1852 election, in which his rival was none other than his old commanding officer, Winfield Scott (the Whig candidate when the party did not nominate Fillmore). In the event, Pierce thrashed his opponent, carrying twenty-seven states to Scott's four to become America's fourteenth president.

After one of the biggest margins of victory in American presidential history, it might be assumed that Pierce started his presidency in high spirits, but that was not the case. Pierce and his wife had already experienced the deaths of two of their children, and now, in a train crash two months before his inauguration, their last surviving child, an eleven-year-old son, was crushed to death in the derailment. Pierce was devastated.

Pierce had always liked a drink, so it comes as no surprise that such an overwhelming blow caused him to drink more heavily. While this was a very human response to tragedy, a drunk president, reeling from crushing loss, is not what any country needs in a leader. Pierce couldn't turn to his wife for consolation as she, too, was in deep mourning and prone to 'melancholy' (depression). This was the backdrop to a presidency that was seeing ever greater demands for a resolution of the tensions between the slave-owning states and the free states. Only a man at the top of his game could hope to salvage the situation, and Pierce simply wasn't up to the job.

31. Franklin Pierce Was Seen as a Traitor by the North

President Pierce confronted an impossible situation. While today we can all agree that slavery is wrong, the South, even if it secretly agreed with the moral principle, faced colossal upheaval. Its society and its economy were based on slavery. Since slave labour was an essential component of the economy, in the event of abolition the South would suffer severe recession, if not total collapse. Putting it another way, what politician would vote for that?

The Southern politicians dug in their heels as they desperately tried to maintain a status quo which, with every passing year, was looking more and more archaic. While there was cold political and business logic to their position, I do not want to shy away from the terrible levels of racism that existed. The black slaves were regarded as less than human; their 'rights' did not enter into it; they were mere chattels to be bought and sold.

Meanwhile the North's industrialisation was gaining more and more momentum as its population increased, thanks to regular injections of largely white immigrants.

In the middle of this was Franklin Pierce who, surprisingly for a northern lawyer, tended towards pro-slavery but more than anything wanted to avoid war. By signing the Kansas–Nebraska Act, which reneged on stopping slavery in some of the American territories, he was backsliding on what had been previously agreed, a big victory for the slave-owning states.

But ultimately everything he did only further polarised the sides. The stage was set for the secession of the South.

32. James Buchanan Was Poised to Do Great Things

The early life of James Buchanan sets him up to be one of the great stories in American presidential history. Another leader to have been born in a log cabin (was it the must-have start of the era?), Buchanan had served in his youth as a volunteer in the successful defence of Baltimore during the War of 1812. So although he had a war record, Buchanan was the only American president to have served in the armed forces without achieving officer rank.

Buchanan's first love was politics. He started in the House of Representatives and later became a senator. He was America's Minister to Russia under Andrew Jackson and, later under James Polk, he was Secretary of State. Later still, Franklin Pierce made him Ambassador to Britain.

In addition to his talents, Buchanan had the connections to enhance his political clout. He was a Freemason and rose to high rank in the Pennsylvania state organisation. It seemed that fate and hard work destined the man to become president and further thanks to his decades of political experience, to be a great one.

The real race in 1856 was between the Democrats and the Republicans, the two parties that would dominate American politics ever after. By the time of the election, Pierce was reviled, seen as a traitor by the North. Still recovering from the death of his son and attending to the needs of his depressed wife, Pierce chose not to run for re-election.

Prior to the election Buchanan had been abroad as Ambassador to Britain and had not been involved in some of the more recent legislative moves that inflamed the slavery question. As a result he had a broader appeal than some of his rivals. He became the new Democratic candidate, comfortably beating the Republican John Fremont. Buchanan took nineteen states to the Republican's eleven. By the mid-nineteenth century a pattern of voting for parties, rather than candidates, was emerging. On a number of occasions past presidents had run as third candidates for a minor party and barely made a dent in the electoral votes.

Buchanan replaced the pro-slavery Pierce but inherited all the same problems. Abraham Lincoln is usually regarded as the greatest president in US history, having resolved the issue of slavery once and for all while preserving the Union by winning a civil war. If those are the two things that make Lincoln a president to admire, then Buchanan created the crisis that Lincoln had to solve. So, up against some fierce competition (Madison, Fillmore and Pierce), Buchanan is often considered to be the worst president in American history.

The issue of slavery has been cropping up regularly in the first third of this book, so it wasn't as if Buchanan was suddenly responsible for the tensions; but, as we will see, in his attempts to bring about a workable compromise, all his political skills seemed to desert him and he managed only to alienate both sides of the argument. Buchanan's presidency was one of missed opportunities.

33. THE CIVIL WAR ALL BUT STARTED UNDER BUCHANAN

In his inaugural speech, James Buchanan, the fifteenth president, said two interesting things: that he would not seek a second term and that he would abide by the US Supreme court ruling on Dred Scott versus Sandford. The verdict came just a few days later and it was dynamite. The US Supreme Court ruled that African Americans, whether enslaved or free, could not be American citizens and, therefore, could not sue in federal court. This was bad enough, but it went on to say that the federal government had no power to regulate slavery in the federal territories (as opposed to the states). The South was delighted; the North was outraged.

Civil war had basically already started in Kansas in what became known as 'Bleeding Kansas', where pro-slavery and anti-slavery groups were waging guerrilla war on one another. This rumbled on until 1861, when the American Civil War formally started. With regard to Dred Scott and the situation in Kansas, Buchanan said that the judiciary would make the right decisions, which made him look like a bystander watching events unfurl in his own presidency.

Unusually, Buchanan did show decisiveness when it looked like Utah, under the Mormons, was set to break away from the Union, and he sent troops in to resolve the issue. No major battles were fought, but brute military strength brought the Mormon community to heel.

In the end it was Buchanan's garbled policy of appeasement with the southern states that lit the touchpaper for all-out war. Before he left office, all government military posts and forts in the seceding states were lost, with a few exceptions, most notably Fort Sumter in South Carolina. Buchanan made an unofficial agreement with the state that in return for no interference he would not reinforce the garrison. Critically (and unforgivably), Buchanan did not inform the Charleston commander of the agreement, and on 26 December 1860 the commander violated this unknown pact by moving his command to Fort Sumter. Southerners responded that Buchanan should remove the reinforcements, while northerners demanded support for the garrison. On 5 January 1861, Buchanan sent a civilian steamship to carry reinforcements and supplies to Fort Sumter. Four days later, South Carolina coastal batteries opened fire on the ship as it approached. The ship withdrew and returned to New York.

As a result, Buchanan was attacked by the South for breaking his agreement and trying to reinforce a fort that he had pledged he wouldn't, while the North criticised the humiliating retreat from the South Carolina batteries. After this Buchanan thought a policy of doing nothing was best. This was the situation that was playing out as Abraham Lincoln was assuming office.

On his death bed, Buchanan said, 'History will vindicate my memory,' but, like most of his presidential judgments, he was wrong about this, too. While it is a matter of some debate that he was the very worst president, he is certainly near the bottom of the list.

34. The 1860 Election Started a War

While the title of this fact isn't strictly true, the battle lines of a real war were being drawn during the 1860 election. For the first time there were four parties, all of which garnered a serious number of votes. Abraham Lincoln was the Republican candidate, but the Democrats had split along the fault line of slavery, now with a Democratic and a Southern Democratic candidate. Finally there was the Constitutional Union Party composed of former Whigs, 'Know Nothings' and a few Southern Democrats who wanted to avoid secessionism over the slavery issue.

Although he garnered less than 40 per cent of the popular vote, Lincoln easily won enough electoral votes to become the sixteenth president. He won no southern states as all of them had voted for the Southern Democratic candidate, John Breckinridge, on a platform of pro-slavery and secession. Lincoln, by contrast, campaigned overtly on an anti-slavery expansion platform, and he did not recognise the right to secession by the southern states.

(It's worth pausing to reflect on a legal point. Abraham Lincoln's refusal to accept secession as lawful has an interesting echo in America's history. It has been playfully suggested by some British historians that 'secede' is exactly what the American colonies did with Britain in 1776. It's the same principle. So if Lincoln was correct, it means that America's initial break from Britain was also illegal.)

After decades of ignoring the issue of slavery and arguing over federal versus state legislative powers, there had been enough talk. The North clearly believed it was time for the South to change and do things the northern way. The South, meanwhile, had had enough of being dictated to by the federal government. There was no longer any way out of the situation. The two sides were too entrenched for further discussion or compromise. The only solution was a civil war to determine if the Union would prevail.

Following Lincoln's inauguration in March of 1861, Fort Sumter was, once again, the flashpoint (in April) for hostilities. With the Union garrison running low on food, the batteries of South Carolina's defences fired on the isolated island. The Union forces surrendered on the second day. There had been no casualties on either side during the bombardment (although several men were mortally wounded due to an accident with gunpowder afterwards). Earlier, in January, seven of the southern slave states had seceded from the Union and declared themselves to be the Confederate States of America: this was the first battle of the American Civil War and was a bloodless victory for the South.

The battle seemed only to whet the appetite of both sides for more military action. By the end of the war close to three-quarters of a million Americans would be dead, with huge swathes of the South stripped of materials, resources and infrastructure. This was to be the single most destructive war ever waged on American soil. It even claimed the life of a president.

35. Jefferson Davis was the 'Other' President during the Civil War

The history of the papacy is horribly complex. During the Middle Ages there were often two popes claiming to be 'the Pope', and sometimes there were three. It was only after decades had passed that historians would reach a consensus as to which was the 'true pope'. You may be wondering how medieval popes got into a book about American presidents, but it's a useful analogy. Today President Jefferson Davis is not included on the list of American presidents (nor are any of the names from the list of presidents prior to Washington, as mentioned in Fact 1). As with the list of popes, there seems to have been an unspoken agreement to prune any anomalies from the list to make it as seamless as possible.

As the President of the Confederacy, Jefferson Davis is not accepted as an American president, and just as the North did not recognise Jefferson Davis, the South did not recognise Abraham Lincoln. But it seems fair and sensible to devote one fact to the one Confederate president.

Davis served in the US Army for eleven years, eventually rising to the rank of colonel. He fought in both the Black Hawk War and the Mexican–American War. There was never any doubt about his commitment to the military. He served diligently in multiple senior governmental positions and was Franklin Pierce's Secretary of War. Davis even argued against secession. He wasn't simply a traitor-in-waiting.

Davis was not instrumental in the start of the war, but when his home state of Mississippi seceded he expected to serve in the Confederate Army. He owned over a hundred slaves on his Mississippi plantation and was the embodiment of the slave-owning gentry.

But Davis was an able politician as well, so instead of joining the army of the South, he was voted in as the President of the Confederacy.

Davis was a capable administrator but he faced some insurmountable problems. The North was far more industrialised and had about three-and-a-half times the population of the South. The agrarian and slave-based economy of the South was inefficient and couldn't match the production capabilities of the North. Davis mistakenly tried to defend all areas equally, spreading his limited resources too thinly; as the war ground on, he had no option but to keep printing money, which led to rampant inflation. Further, Davis failed to recognise the needs of the general population, and food shortages led to riots in 1863. Possibly his worst mistake was to assume for himself the role of commander-in-chief, waiting until January of 1865 to appoint General Robert E. Lee. By then, it was too late.

When the inevitable happened and the South finally surrendered in April of 1865, Davis made no public statement about the peace terms. After the war and the abolition of slavery, he became a slavery apologist, refusing to admit that it was an abhorrent crime. He remained extremely popular in the South, and his funeral in 1889 was attended by thousands.

36. THE GETTYSBURG ADDRESS GOT SECOND BILLING

The Confederate capital of Richmond, Virginia was only a little over 100 miles from the US capital of Washington D.C., and the two cities would both see numerous bloody battles. Tens of thousands on both sides were killed or wounded at Gettysburg, but the battle stopped Confederate attempts to invade the North. It was seen as the beginning of the end of both the war and the Confederate war machine, but it had been achieved at a terrible price.

On 19 November 1863, a crowd gathered to dedicate the Soldiers' National Cemetery in Gettysburg, Pennsylvania. Everyone had come to see Edward Everett, one of the great public speakers of the age, give a dramatic speech. They weren't disappointed: it was a two-hour tour de force.

When President Lincoln got up to make 'a few appropriate remarks', he spoke for only a few minutes, and the significance of what he said was largely lost on the crowd in front of him. However, once his words had been printed and distributed, Lincoln's 'Gettysburg Address' was destined to become one of the greatest speeches in history. Here it is in all its simple glory:

> Fourscore and seven years ago our fathers brought forth on this continent a new nation, conceived in liberty and dedicated to the proposition that all men are created equal. Now we are engaged in a great civil war, testing whether that nation or any nation so conceived and so dedicated can long endure.
>
> We are met on a great battlefield of that war. We have come to dedicate a portion of that field as a final resting place for those who here gave their lives that that nation might live. It is altogether fitting and proper

that we should do this. But in a larger sense, we cannot
dedicate, we cannot consecrate, we cannot hallow this
ground. The brave men, living and dead who struggled
here have consecrated it far above our poor power to
add or detract.

The world will little note nor long remember what
we say here, but it can never forget what they did
here. It is for us the living rather to be dedicated here
to the unfinished work which they who fought here
have thus far so nobly advanced. It is rather for us to
be here dedicated to the great task remaining before
us—that from these honored dead we take increased
devotion to that cause for which they gave the last full
measure of devotion—that we here highly resolve that
these dead shall not have died in vain, that this nation
under God shall have a new birth of freedom, and that
government of the people, by the people, for the people
shall not perish from the earth.

Everett's speech is now forgotten, but what Lincoln
did in around 250 words explained the stakes of a
civil war, honoured (we're back to British spelling) the
war dead and stiffened the resolve of the people who
were living through the bloodiest period in American
history.

37. ABRAHAM LINCOLN FOUGHT A WAR TO SOLVE A PROBLEM

The war was well under way before Lincoln was able to put together a winning team of generals. The Confederates had inspiring and efficient military leaders like 'Stone Wall' Jackson and General Lee, naturally gifted, aggressive and decisive military leaders. Lincoln had competent, well-meaning but decidedly average generals such as Meade and McClellan. It wasn't until later in the war when the more dynamic and ruthless Union generals Grant and Sherman took a pragmatic (and brutal) approach by destroying the South's economy and infrastructure that victory was finally achieved.

The Emancipation Proclamation of 1863 led to the inclusion of the Thirteenth Amendment to the Constitution. It permanently outlawed slavery and is seen as Lincoln's greatest achievement; certainly it is the most morally satisfying. But the devastation caused by the war left Lincoln with many problems. He recognised how badly the South had been damaged by the fighting and understood that, if the southern states were to be punished for their actions, it would only lead to lingering resentment (although it's fair to say that even though Lincoln tried to avoid this, there is still – today – lingering resentment in the South).

1864 was an election year, and despite the fact Lincoln was waging a war and did not have a unified northern government behind him, he still had the energy and the mental capacity to manage both the war and his own re-election. As the war drew to a close, some angry northern politicians wanted to punish the South, but Lincoln's return to office gave him the mandate he needed to conduct the post-war years in a peaceful and generous way.

In the South, the period from the end of the war in 1865 to 1877 is referred to as the Reconstruction Era, a time when the economy was forced not only to move away from its dependence on slavery, but also a period of federal investment in the rebuilding of infrastructure and repairing of extensive damage wrought by the Union armies.

And Lincoln's reward for reaching out to the South, for exercising nuance, flexibility and reason? The Confederate spy John Wilkes Booth shot the president in the back of the head as he sat watching a play in the Ford Theatre on 11 April 1865. The North went into deep mourning as Lincoln's body travelled around on a special funeral train decked in black bunting and ribbons. Wherever it stopped, thousands came to pay their respects. When it couldn't stop, they simply stood with bowed heads as the train passed by.

Lincoln's Secretary of War, Edwin Stanton, was there when the president was pronounced dead. He saluted and said, 'Now he belongs to the ages.' Stanton's words were prophetic. When historians debate the greatest American president, Abraham Lincoln is always on the shortlist and usually wins the argument. It is a tragic irony that America's greatest president was the first to be assassinated, gunned down by one of his fellow countrymen.

38. Andrew Johnson Tried to Rebuild the Nation

With the death of Lincoln, Vice President Andrew Johnson became the seventeenth President of the United States. He was a southerner who came from such a poor background that he and his brother were sold as indentured servants. They eventually escaped, but the hardships continued, and even though Johnson never received any formal schooling, he taught himself to read.

A southern politician in the Civil War, Johnson was unique as he was the only US Representative from the South to retain his seat after the secession of his state, so Johnson was a southerner who was on the Union side. You would think that the clamour against him would come from the South – a traitor to the cause – but in fact, it was the radical members of his own party in the North who were his greatest opponents.

Johnson's presidency is usually viewed through the lens of Reconstruction. That is fair as it was during this period that the resources of the country were put into rebuilding the infrastructure of the South. However, some Republicans thought that too much money was being spent on areas that just a year or so earlier saw rebels doing their best to kill Union soldiers and destroy the Union.

Jefferson Davis was imprisoned for two years, bailed and lived in Canada before being formally pardoned by Johnson in 1868. The president was criticised for not bringing to trial as many southerners as he might have done, but this was a wise move. To perennially punish the South would not allow the wounds of civil war to heal; however, the friction between political logic and political reality got Johnson into deep trouble. The situation became so polarised and so explosive that in 1866 he broke from the Republican Party.

The cause of much of the problem stemmed from the Civil Rights Act, which Johnson vetoed (as not all states were represented, he felt he could not sign it) and, for the first time ever, Congress overrode a presidential veto on a major bill. As a result, Johnson had to seek support from the northern and southern Democrats. The president was at war with his own party.

It should come as no surprise that a call for impeachment was made against the president. The charges had to do with Johnson replacing the Secretary of War (in doing so he had violated the Tenure of Office Act). According to the letter of the law, Johnson's action justified impeachment proceedings, but in reality the charges were merely an excuse to prosecute him for the matters outlined above.

The impeachment trial lasted nearly three months. Thirty-five voted 'guilty' and nineteen 'not guilty'. However, the Constitution dictates that a two-thirds majority must be achieved, and the Senate fell short by one vote. Johnson was coming to the end of his presidency and nobody wanted him on their ticket for the coming election, so the rest of the proceedings were allowed to wither away. Johnson had avoided impeachment by the narrowest of margins.

39. WILLIAM SEWARD BOUGHT ALASKA

Andrew Johnson is forever linked to the American Civil War and the subsequent Reconstruction, but there was another key aspect of his presidency which, at the time, was seen as yet one more mistake. It turned out to be one of the shrewdest moves any American president has ever made.

Johnson's Secretary of State was William Seward, and he had been busy talking to the Russian government. Russia was then about as far removed from America as you could get, but Seward's intention was to buy some of its real estate located on the North American continent. The area in question was Alaska. There was some interesting chicanery in the initial negotiations: for example, Joseph S. Wilson, the Commissioner of the General Land Office, said that all the imperial powers were interested in the land (they weren't) and that Alaska's climate had 'a high range of climatic temperature ... [with a] wonderful current of warm water'.

But it was Seward who made the decision, and his purchase of Alaska for $7.2 million became known as 'Seward's Folly'.

However, as the years rolled by the advantages of the purchase became apparent. In the last years of the nineteenth century, gold was discovered in Alaska. Then in the twentieth century, large oil and natural gas deposits were identified. Finally, the acquisition meant that the US had a strategically important border with Russia (later, the Soviet Union and then, Russia again). What had initially seemed a bad deal turned out to have been one of the best purchases in American history.

40. Ulysses S. Grant Was a General and a President

Including those from humble backgrounds, most presidents tended to be learned men of letters, lawyers or grizzled war veterans. Grant fell into the last category. In his youth he enjoyed painting, and a few of his works are still in existence, but if Grant ever had any ambitions in that direction, they were repressed when he was sent to a military academy. An average student, he graduated in 1839 and spent the next thirty years in the army before leading the Union forces to victory in the American Civil War.

While Grant was a war hero in the North, he was despised in the South. He was a strong, rather than automatic, choice for presidential candidate in 1868, an election that bore the scars of the war. Texas, Mississippi and Virginia had yet to be reinstated in the Union and, as such, could not vote (a fact that helped Grant). Johnson had been loved by the South but had faced impeachment, so his candidacy might have persuaded voters to turn their backs on the Republicans. Grant, however, was virtually the exact opposite of Johnson, and his selection reinvigorated the Republican chances of regaining the White House. For the first time in a long time it was just a two-horse race. As no other parties were represented, it was the Republicans versus the Democrats – so in a way, the election of 1868 can be seen as the first 'modern' American election.

The Democrats, despite working with Johnson, decided to go with a new face, that of Horatio Seymour. Many people in history have assumed a mock façade of modesty about elections and nominations, usually with one eye on history, but Seymour genuinely didn't want to run, which is a problem when you are the

Democratic nominee for president. The campaigns split along racial lines, with Grant, due to his quite literal fight against slavery, seen as the 'black' (a far more pejorative term was used at the time) candidate, and Seymour seen as the 'white' candidate.

Grant knew that, although he had name recognition, he was not a veteran politician, and he pounced on the opportunity to have House Speaker Schuyler Colfax run as his vice president. They were both relatively young and complemented each other's skill sets and experience.

The election turned out to be close in terms of the popular vote, with Seymour winning a little over 47 per cent. However, a quirk in the rules of American elections that crops up again and again meant that the result of the popular vote did not equate to the resulting electoral votes. Of these, Grant got 214 to Seymour's 80.

As plans were taking shape for the inauguration of the eighteenth president, Grant revealed that he would not ride in a carriage to the Capitol with President Johnson. Johnson then (and unusually) decided not to attend the ceremony. In the event, the inaugural parade included eight full divisions of the US Army, the largest contingent ever to have been at a presidential inauguration.

41. Grant Found the Wild West too Wild

Ulysses was not Grant's first name. He was born Hiram Ulysses Grant and his name was accidentally changed by a congressman who thought Ulysses was his first name and that Grant's mother's maiden name (Simpson) was his middle name. Grant didn't bother to correct the mistake so has gone down in history with the wrong name.

Naming issues to one side, when Grant came to office the Reconstruction of the South was still ongoing, and Grant was in the unusual position of using tax dollars to fix areas that he had destroyed in the first place. However, there were apparently no hard feelings on the part of the veteran general who, to his credit, assiduously continued to rebuild the South.

Somewhat counter-intuitively, Grant also reduced the amount of settler expansion into native lands. The white settlement and extension of these lands and the accompanying removal and resettlement of Native Americans had been the standard government policy for nearly forty years, so it is somewhat startling to learn that a general felt squeamish about the practice when so many presidents without military records had happily carried out what amounted to ethnic cleansing.

In regard to what had been accepted American policy Grant said, 'Wars of extermination ... are demoralizing and wicked.' In an attempt to more fairly and effectively organise native tribes under government protection, he created the Board of Indian Commissioners. This was supposed to reduce the level of corruption and incompetence while also teaching the natives Western civilisation. The board was not entirely successful, but it was a step in the right direction and a remarkably tolerant gesture in an age when the white man was thought to have total superiority over Native Americans. Unfortunately, the peaceful coexistence that Grant's decisions had fostered didn't last throughout his two presidential terms. The wholesale slaughter of buffalo on the Great Plains and the discovery of gold in the Black Hills of the north-west once again triggered war between the settlers and the Native Americans. However, it is fair to say that this confrontation was due largely to the greed of the settlers rather than official government policy.

Grant's relations with the Native Americans were not the only area where he showed unusual restraint for an old war horse. The Caribbean islands, an area where America was flexing its naval muscles, were seen as a prime target for further overseas expansion. The specific country of interest was the Dominican Republic. Many thought invading the island would result 'only' in a short, sharp conflict that America had to win. While this was the likely outcome, Grant again chose peace. He sent a commission to the island to discuss a potential annexation treaty, which was seriously considered by the Dominican government. In the back of his mind Grant hoped that the island could be an option for ex-slaves, an opportunity to live away from the still powerful southern landowners. Eventually the whole scheme was stalled by Congress and came to nothing.

42. Grant Faced Economic and Corruption Scandals

Grant lived in an era of 'Wild West' expansion and with that came speculation and risk. It was also the time when the American Dream (a concept not widely popularised until the 1930s) was starting to take root: if you had guts and determination, you could succeed economically and rise up the social ladder in America. However, the early concept embraced risk, and not every risk pays off.

In the late 1860s, Grant sought to strengthen the dollar and return to a gold standard. When news of this leaked to the inner circles of finance, those in the know began to buy gold, hence artificially inflating its price. On realising that this was a ploy by financial institutions, Grant decided to teach them a lesson and began selling treasury gold, which sent the price plummeting and ruined the corrupt profiteers. It was a victory for Grant in the world of finance – but it wasn't always like that.

The group behind the inflation of gold prices became known as the Gold Ring. A few years later there was a Whisky Ring, when some unscrupulous Republican politicians were skimming off the revenues generated through liquor sales. Even the humble postal service was not immune when remote postal routes were won through bribes and kickbacks in a ruse known as the Star Route Postal Ring, which persisted until the 1880s. This was a period of rapid industrial growth known as the Gilded Age. There were huge opportunities to make money, but there was also widespread corruption.

Grant was a straightforward military man and had no interest in enriching himself through corruption, but the government system he presided over was riddled with scandals throughout his two terms.

In 1873 Jay Cooke & Company, a US bank and brokerage firm, collapsed when it failed to sell a railway bond. While railway investments had always been a risky business, they had always attracted big money. This collapse precipitated a financial crisis that became known as the 'Panic of 1873', which was followed by the 'Long Depression'. About a quarter of the 350-plus railways went bankrupt. Grant continued to shore up the value of the dollar and even set up the Civil Service Commission in a vain attempt to reduce corruption. It didn't work, but it is clear Grant knew what the problem was and attempted to tackle it.

Grant attended the International Exhibition of Arts, Manufactures and Products of the Soil and Mine, which was known by everyone (except the organisers) as the Centennial International Exhibition of 1876. This was a chance to celebrate 100 years of an independent America … except that in 1876 there wasn't a lot to celebrate. The country was in an economic slump, Custer and the cream of his Seventh Cavalry had been massacred at Little Bighorn, the South was still in recovery and government corruption seemed endemic. Grant had won the war but lost the peace and decided not to run in the 1876 election. Instead the Republican candidate was Rutherford B. Hayes.

43. The Wrong Person Won the 1876 Election

While it was the Republican Rutherford B. Hayes who won the 1876 election and became the nineteenth President of the United States, the Democrat Samuel J. Tilden should have been the winner.

The election was (arguably) the closest and most contentious in American history, with so many twists and turns that it seemed almost anybody could have won. For starters, it was not yet enframed in law (rather just tradition) that a president didn't run for more than two terms. Grant was told that he had enough Republican support to be nominated for a third time, but the Republicans (and Grant) knew that so many economic problems had occurred over the previous eight years that he was unlikely to win. So Grant, a decent and honourable man, stepped aside and retired from both politics and the military at the age of just fifty-four.

Meanwhile, the Democratic candidate was an anti-corruption zealot, who had managed to uncover enough evidence of corruption to get a judge impeached. Mentions were made in the previous fact of the Gold Ring and the Whiskey Ring, among others, but Tilden managed to uncover and end both the Tweed Ring and the Canal Ring (America, at this time, had more corrupt 'rings' than the *Lord of the Rings*). After years of economic woes and financial mismanagement, America liked the look of the Democratic reformer.

While both parties wanted reform, the argument chimed better with the Democrats, who hadn't been in power for some time, and Tilden had genuine credentials in this area. The Republicans replied with supporters shouting a crass reminder from the civil war: 'Not every Democrat was a rebel, but every rebel was a Democrat.'

When Election Day came there were disputes about ballots. To aid illiterate voters, symbols were often used, some of which were considered to be intentionally provocative. The use of Abraham Lincoln's image as the Republican symbol in states such as Florida and Louisiana were said to be the reason why Hayes managed to squeak in. Meanwhile, Colorado became the 38th state in August of the same year and claimed insufficient time or money to organise an election. The state legislature selected the state's electors, who in turn gave their three electoral votes to the Republicans.

Hayes won 4,034,311 of the popular votes compared to Tilden's 4,288,546, so while Tilden won the popular vote 50.9 per cent to 47.9 per cent, thanks again to the peculiarities of the American electoral system, he carried only seventeen states to Hayes' twenty-one. Hayes had 185 electoral votes to Tilden's 184.

After this counter-intuitive mess of an election, in January 1877 Congress brought into law a fifteen-member Electoral Commission to determine who had truly won the election and to avoid constitutional crises in the future. The election of 1876 was a shameful display of cynical manipulation by both parties, however the unusual rules of the American election system meant that the man with fewer popular votes won the election.

44. RUTHERFORD B. HAYES WAS A MEDIOCRE PRESIDENT

A few months into Hayes' presidency, the east erupted in an industrial dispute known as the Great Railroad Strike of 1877. Maryland, Pennsylvania, Illinois and Missouri rose up after rail workers' wages were cut for the third time in a year. The strikers stopped the movement of freight trains and were taking a toll on the fragile economy. Hayes responded by raising militias and sending in the army. This led to skirmishes in places such as Pittsburgh, where more than twenty died in one clash, but Hayes' use of the army eventually crushed all opposition.

Hayes also ended the period of Reconstruction in the South. It was now more than a decade after the war and the costs had been staggering. Both he and the Democrats had campaigned on ending it in the 1876 election.

Overall Hayes is a rather bland footnote of a president. He didn't plunge the country into chaos, but neither did he do anything of such note that it has echoed down the generations ... except, that is, in Paraguay.

In the late nineteenth century, South America was a continent always on the brink of war. However, a crisis in 1878 between Paraguay and Argentina over disputed territory was resolved not by war, but by a neutral party, who just happened to be President Hayes. Hayes saw the Paraguayan claim as the more valid and gave the country 60 per cent of its current territory. Rutherford B. Hayes is largely forgotten in his own country but is fondly remembered in Paraguayan history.

45. James A. Garfield Served with Distinction in the Civil War

When Garfield was made Colonel of the 42nd Ohio Infantry regiment in the summer of 1861, there was just one problem: it didn't exist. Garfield was expected to fill the ranks with everyone he knew, which he promptly did. He was eventually promoted to the rank of brigadier general and personally led troops in the bitter cold of the Battle of Middle Creek. He was under fire for most of a day at the bloody Battle of Shiloh and ended up having to convalesce at home when he contracted jaundice. From this we can conclude that Garfield was a brave man who took his responsibilities seriously. This is further reflected in his diligent service from 1863 to 1880 as a member of the US House of Representatives.

Garfield suffered one notable setback in the Crédit Mobilier scandal of 1872, when it was revealed that some government officials were voting in favour of proposals for new railroads in return for stocks in the ventures – basically, cash for votes. Garfield was implicated, but he denied the charges. The revelations eventually subsided, and Garfield was selected as the Republican candidate for the 1880 presidential election against the Democrat Winfield Hancock.

In the course of the campaign, the Republicans reminded the nation that the Democrats were the ones who had triggered the Civil War, even though old wounds were starting to heal. Equally, the Democrats were happy to remind everyone that Garfield had been caught exchanging votes for railway stocks. Then the Republicans changed tack and began to portray the Democrats as unsympathetic to labour unions and the working man – a bit rich when, only a few years earlier, the Republican President Hayes had deployed the army to crush industrial strikes.

Everyone was anxious that the 1880 election should run much more smoothly than the nightmare election of 1876. The electorate was certainly engaged, as 78 per cent of eligible voters cast a ballot, but once again it was close. Of nearly 9 million popular votes cast, there were only 2,000 votes in it, with Garfield achieving the slightly greater number. Both candidates carried nineteen states each. However, it was where those votes were cast and which states were won that determined the distribution of the electoral votes. In the end Garfield had 214 electoral votes to Hancock's 155.

Garfield's inauguration as America's twentieth president took place on a day that was cold even by Washington standards; with snow on the ground, attendance was low. His inaugural speech had a powerful opening:

> We stand to-day upon an eminence which overlooks a hundred years of national life—a century crowded with perils, but crowned with the triumphs of liberty and law. Before continuing the onward march let us pause on this height for a moment to strengthen our faith and renew our hope by a glance at the pathway along which our people have travelled.

Like Lincoln, Garfield was a gifted orator. Eventually he was to share another similarity with Lincoln.

46. Charles Guiteau Was the Most Dangerous Lawyer in American History

Charles Guiteau was an abysmal lawyer whose track record was terrible – well, short – as he seems to have argued only one case in court. But none of this prevented Guiteau from having a high opinion of himself. He thought that an obscure speech he'd written for President Garfield (originally written for Grant) had led to Garfield's victory and, as such, had earned Guiteau a place at the table. He was dismissed comprehensively by Garfield's Secretary of State, James G. Blaine.

His many bizarre actions (one among them was that he joined a religious cult but was eventually thrown out) led to family attempts to get him committed to an insane asylum in the 1870s. That he had mental health issues was in no doubt. Nevertheless, Guiteau was allowed to go about his business as if he were able to conduct a normal life. Unfortunately, even in the 1880s, anybody in America, including an insane lawyer, could buy a gun. Guiteau chose a five-round-cylinder British Bulldog revolver.

Guiteau was planning to assassinate the president, and, having acquired the gun, he spent the next few weeks in target practice. He stalked Garfield for months and wrote a letter saying that the president should fire Blaine; the letter was ignored. So he wrote to General Sherman asking for protection from the mob he assumed would gather after he had killed the president. Nobody took any notice. Guiteau was even thorough enough to take a tour of the local jail to see where he would likely be imprisoned.

On 2 July 1881, Guiteau decided to make his move on President Garfield when he arrived at the Sixth Street Station in Washington D.C. On the day, Garfield was accompanied by his two sons and two members of the Cabinet. There were no bodyguards or security of any kind. Guiteau simply stepped up behind the president and fired two shots into his back.

After the first bullet, Garfield's arms flew up, and he was heard to say, 'My God, what is that?'

Guiteau tried to leave the scene but was immediately apprehended by a passing policeman. Garfield was mortally wounded, and although doctors told him he would not survive the night, they were wrong; over the next six weeks, his condition fluctuated. The problem was finding the bullet still lodged in him. Using unsterilized fingers and instruments, doctors poked and probed. (The critical role of sterilization would be discovered only ten years later.) Alexander Graham Bell got involved and invented a metal detector to find the bullet, but it didn't occur to anyone that there would be interference from the metal bed frame, and the bullet was never located. Just a few months into his presidency, Garfield died of infection from his wounds on 19 September 1881.

Guiteau continued to display mental derangement when he decided during his trial for murder to run for president in 1884. His plans were curtailed when he was hanged on 30 June 1882.

47. THE NEW YORK CUSTOMS HOUSE COULD PICK PRESIDENTS

Of course the statement in this fact's title is, technically speaking, not true. The votes of the people determined who was president ... but who picked the candidates? Late nineteenth-century American politics (in both major parties) were awash with scandal and corruption. Political machines created slush funds to back the man most compliant with their wishes. If you think it's bad nowadays, this is nothing compared to America in the 1870s and 80s.

One president who was so compromised that he had even run the notoriously corrupt New York Customs House, was Chester A. Arthur. He had achieved his post by serving the party machine but was later removed by President Hayes, who wanted to reform the spoils system (a system of patronage).

Arthur was Garfield's vice president and had made it to that position by greasing the right palms at the right time. It would therefore be easy to think that when Garfield died and Arthur became the twenty-first president, he was poised to sit at the trough of money coming from the political machines and gulp it down like the corrupt swine he was. If proof of his corruption is required, let's just say that he was earning around $50,000 a year in the early 1870s – roughly $880,000 in today's money, far more than anyone else in government. But once he became president, Arthur clearly had an attack of conscience and stunned everyone.

Rather than allowing his new position to drive him into further greedy moves, Arthur used his considerable insider information to create a reform bill which dealt with all the major problems around corruption. Called the Pendleton Civil Service Reform Act of 1883, it was passed through Congress and signed into law by Arthur himself. It established the Civil Service Commission to ensure that candidates for government jobs had to pass examinations and that government employees were protected against removal for political reasons. It broke the power of the political cliques and reinvigorated the civil service.

This was political dynamite, and Arthur must have known that the bill was a grand-scale betrayal of everyone he had worked with up until becoming president. While the Pendleton Act was Arthur's centrepiece, it was not his only important piece of legislation. He was determined to reduce tariffs, even going against his own party and reaching out to the Democrats to pass the Tariff Act of 1883. Arthur was also the first president to enact a federal immigration law, which in this case restricted paupers, criminals and the insane from entering the country. This was a tacit acknowledgement that the era of mass immigration from Europe had worked so well that America could now afford to be pickier about whom it admitted.

Arthur, then in his mid-fifties, chose not to run for a second term of office. He was offered an opportunity to run for the Senate but declined, deciding to turn his back on politics. He left office in 1885 and died in the winter of 1886.

48. GROVER CLEVELAND WAS MORE THAN AN ANOMALY

Grover Cleveland is not one of the giants of American history, but if there's one thing people know about him it's that he was the only president to have served non-consecutive terms in office. Unusual as this is, there was more to this man that history remembers with the wrong name (he was christened Stephen Grover Cleveland).

The quirks of the American electoral system once again explain the reason for Cleveland's non-consecutive claim to fame. He was the winner of the popular vote for president three times, in 1884, 1888 and 1892: it was just that in 1888 the votes fell in the wrong states to allow for an electoral majority, so it was only natural for him to try a third time. But on his first attempt in 1884, he only just squeaked into the White House as the twenty-second president.

Cleveland was the Democratic bright spark during a period of more than seventy years when Republican candidates almost always won the elections. Their run started with Abraham Lincoln and, with the exception of Woodrow Wilson's tenure from 1913 to 1921, continued until Franklin D. Roosevelt became president in 1933. Cleveland's appeal was simple: he was a reformer. He was seen as one of a new generation of politicians untarnished by the old political machines. He became the mayor of Buffalo, New York in 1881, and, just a year later, he became the Governor of New York.

The 1884 election was quite a rollercoaster. James Blaine (Garfield's former Secretary of State, who had ignored the letter from Guiteau) was the Republican nominee but had run into trouble with some incriminating letters showing that he had 'sold his influence'. It didn't help that one of his letters ended with the instruction to 'burn this letter', which the opposition Democrats turned into a popular chant. The Republicans hit back that Cleveland was financially supporting a woman and her child – was this an illegitimate child of Cleveland's? Strangely, Cleveland hinted that might well be the case (or that the child could have been his business partner's). Cleveland was applauded for his honesty and the Republicans rolled their eyes in frustration.

Despite all of this, the whole election could well have hung on just one speech by a man who wasn't even running for office. The Reverend Dr Samuel Burchard made an anti-Catholic comment during a Republican meeting; it was promptly picked up by the Democrats and used to stoke resentment in the Irish Catholic community on the East Coast, including the key state of New York, where Cleveland was the governor. In the end, the election hung on New York, which Cleveland won by less than 0.1 per cent, well within a margin of error. It could well have been Burchard's ill-advised comment that had lost the Republicans the election.

This election saw the emergence of the new Equal Rights Party. It was a single-issue party campaigning for women's suffrage; its nominee was the female attorney Belva Ann Lockwood. In addition, for the first time, there was also a Prohibition candidate.

49. Grover Cleveland Was an Honest Liar

After all the honesty and openness reported in the previous fact, Grover Cleveland began his second term, now as the twenty-fourth president, by concealing important personal information from the nation. What started as a bump on the roof of his mouth grew larger, and he was diagnosed with cancer.

Cleveland feared that if it became common knowledge that the president had a tumour in his head, it could cause political and financial chaos in the country, so he did what any politician would do: he covered it up. It is, however, the scale of his deception that was downright ingenious. He told a few people but excluded his own vice president, Adlai Stevenson, from the news.

Cleveland's cover story was a four-day 'fishing trip' where some of 'the crew' consisted of six of the best surgeons in America. They wanted Cleveland to shave off his moustache so they could go in just below the nose, but Cleveland feared that if his signature moustache was defaced, people would realise something was up, so the operation (on a yacht) was conducted through the roof of his mouth. Four days was the minimum time to convalesce.

Despite the fact that so many things could have gone wrong, the operation was a complete success. Present-day oral surgeons have pronounced the surgery to be nothing short of miraculous. Cleveland made a full recovery, the general population was none the wiser, and perhaps most importantly (probably for Cleveland), the moustache remained resplendent and intact.

50. GROVER CLEVELAND WAS A STEADY PAIR OF HANDS

Due to Cleveland's policies being separated by another presidential incumbent (more on him in the next fact), we can see the political thinking of a president over a twelve-year period. What is particularly interesting about Cleveland's viewpoints is how steady they were, how little they changed over time.

Cleveland's policies on foreign affairs and the military centred on defence and non-engagement. While he modernised the army and navy, it was never his plan to use them in anything but a defensive capacity. It was under Cleveland's presidency that the navy got a base at Pearl Harbor in Hawaii.

President Cleveland was a champion of the Dawes Act of 1887, which gave plots of land to individual Native American tribes. It was a sign of the times that this president saw the redistribution of land as a means of lifting the tribes out of poverty and providing opportunities for cultural integration. Although endorsed by a Native American conference, most of the tribes disliked the act. It undermined tribal governments and resulted in even less land for the tribes when individuals sold their share and kept the money.

But the issue over which Cleveland was to have his biggest political battle was the gold versus the silver standard of the US Dollar. Cleveland thought the currency should be pegged to gold; others wanted to inflate the currency by minting more silver coinage (forcing the government to buy more silver to maintain its stock). Even though he was supported by Wall Street and the banks, it was Cleveland's insistence that the country should stick with the gold standard, seen as the 'old way', which led to his political demise.

While James Buchanan was the first bachelor to become president – and he was clearly a confirmed bachelor – Cleveland was unique in that he fell in love, courted and married, all in his first term as president. The twenty-one-year-old Frances Folsom turned the head of the forty-nine-year-old president, the only one to have been married in the White House. Even in those days the age gap was seen as a big one; but it was, by all accounts, a loving marriage, which produced five children. It's interesting to imagine Cleveland having to attend to affairs of state with a toddler wandering around the White House, or an infant waking the president at four in the morning. Their youngest daughter, born in 1903, died as recently as 1995.

Cleveland's second term never recovered from the Panic of 1893, when a stock market crash heralded an era of economic depression. After retiring from office, Cleveland became a trustee of Princeton University. He would occasionally fire off letters to make his political views known to various newspapers or ex-colleagues, but he spent the last decade of his life in relative obscurity.

Cleveland marks a point at which technology does a better job of bringing historical figures to life. Thanks to the primitive recording technology of the times, it's possible to hear him speak on YouTube.

51. Benjamin Harrison Was the First Environmental President

William Henry Harrison (Fact 20) was president for less than two months before he died. He is a curiosity in the list of American presidents, but his legacy lived on in the form of his grandson Benjamin Harrison (they would have met when Benjamin was a boy). Benjamin's great-grandfather (another Benjamin) was even a signatory to the Declaration of Independence. American politics ran through the veins of Benjamin Harrison, the twenty-third President of the United States.

Any grandfather would have been proud of young Benjamin. He became a successful attorney in Indiana, where he was a Presbyterian Church leader. When the Civil War broke out, he enlisted, rose to the rank of brevet brigadier general and led troops in no fewer than nine separate battles.

As we saw in Fact 22, the election of 1888 was a close-run race. Harrison lost the popular vote, but as he had the majority in the larger states, he was able to win because he secured more electoral votes. The Democrats saw things a little differently, accusing the Republicans of electoral fraud and 'irregular ballot practices'. Harrison declared his victory was due to Providence. This annoyed his fellow Republicans, who orchestrated a winning campaign that had less to do with God and far more to do with political horse trading.

Just like his grandfather's inauguration, the weather was terrible on Benjamin's big day. However, unlike William Henry, Benjamin took sensible precautions … like having an umbrella over him when it rained.

Benjamin Harrison was a mediocre president; his four years in office were competent but unexceptional. His greatest achievement was the Land Revision Act of 1891. It sounds dull, but rather wonderfully created America's National Forests (not to be confused with its National Parks, which came later). These tracts of forest and woodland are owned by the federal government for the people. The idea was to preserve areas of natural beauty and resources. It was a very forward thinking piece of legislation.

Harrison also put considerable effort into defending African American Civil Rights. He once said:

> The colored people did not intrude themselves upon us; they were brought here in chains and held in communities where they are now chiefly bound by a cruel slave code ... when and under what conditions is the black man to have a free ballot?

He tried hard to right the wrongs of previous legislation and southern state rulings, but he wasn't in power long enough with enough of a political mandate to make a dent in this most entrenched American issue.

His legislation regarding Native Americans was largely banal, but it was under his presidency that the massacre of Native Americas took place at Wounded Knee. Twenty soldiers of the Seventh Cavalry received Medals of Honor for their actions, a poor decision, which some are trying to revoke more than a century later.

Harrison was a decent man but a largely ineffectual president. His term in office shows that being nice and getting things done rarely go hand-in-hand.

52. THE STAKES WERE HIGH IN THE US PRESIDENTIAL ELECTION OF 1896

By the end of Grover Cleveland's second term, America had been in deep recession for three years. Unemployment was high, there had been violent strikes and the mood was gloomy. Because so much was at stake, there was great interest in the 1896 election (at over 79 per cent, it had one of the highest turnouts ever recorded); and, unsurprisingly, it was the economy that was the key issue.

The two candidates came with very different solutions to the nation's problems. William McKinley (Republican) had his power base in the cities and was seen as a friend of the titans of industry who would build more, make more and push the country out of recession. William Jennings Bryan (Democrat), by contrast, was a big hit with the workers, the rural poor and the South. He wanted inflation, assured the country that the government had more than enough gold and silver to create more wealth, and challenged the business practices of the industrialists.

Both sides had clearly defined policies so that this time there was less need to sling mud and more focus on the issues, with each party taking every opportunity to knock the other's programmes. The Republicans mocked Bryan's economic policies by printing fake dollar bills with Bryan's face on them, saying, 'In God We Trust ... for the Other 53 Cents' (to illustrate their claims that the dollar would devalue).

It was relatively easy to portray Bryan as a religious zealot with little grasp of economics when he made his 'Cross of Gold' speech, which while making a point about the importance of agriculture, came across as ... well ... apocalyptic:

> Burn down your cities and leave our farms, and your cities will spring up again; but destroy our farms, and the grass will grow in the streets of every city in the country.

It was fiery speeches like this that drew the crowds. In 100 days of campaigning, Bryan made 500 speeches and is estimated to have spoken to some 5 million people.

As the candidates were so different in both politics and personalities, McKinley's plan for reaching the electorate was very different. He used trains to transport half-a-million people to meet him, informally, at his home on his front porch.

When election night came, Bryan did very well with his core voters: the South and the rural Midwest voted for him in their millions. However, his fiery rhetoric and economic policies had unsettled too many in the cities and elsewhere. While McKinley didn't win by a landslide, he did win comfortably. Bryan's religious zealotry had been attacked in the campaign, but the opening of McKinley's inaugural speech was also markedly religious:

> I assume the arduous and responsible duties of President of the United States, relying upon the support of my countrymen and invoking the guidance of Almighty God. Our faith teaches that there is no safer reliance than upon the God of our fathers, who has so singularly favored the American people in every national trial.

53. There Was a Spanish-American War

While US military forces had fought innumerable battles against Native Americans and the South during the Civil War period, it had been some time since America had fought a foreign war. However in 1898, when the US warship *Maine* mysteriously exploded and sank in Havana harbour (historians still do not agree exactly what happened), it sparked a short but ferocious war between America and Spain.

Throughout the late nineteenth century, Spain had been losing control of its overseas empire. America was to join the battle after the unpaid Spanish forces, usually with obsolete equipment, had already faced years of fighting with local rebel groups. In this scenario America could flex its muscles against a soft target with little chance of serious retaliation from an ailing European power.

The war, despite its name, wasn't fought either in Spain or America. Instead, American forces landed on islands that were under Spanish influence. The fighting centred around Cuba and Puerto Rico in the Caribbean, as well as thousands of miles away in the Philippines and Guam in the Pacific. America's twenty-fifth president, William McKinley, wasn't itching for a fight, but for years newspapers had been whipping up popular support for American intervention in these weak Spanish colonies. The destruction of the *Maine* increased the pressure until McKinley had no option but to authorise military action, and the army, navy and marines leapt at the chance to fight in their first overseas war for half a century.

The most famous engagement of the war was the Battle of San Juan Hill in Cuba. When the Americans and their Cuban allies attacked a Spanish fort, the Spanish were completely surrounded and outnumbered around 10-1. It was a fight the Americans were never going to lose, but it was in this battle that Theodore Roosevelt and his 'Rough Riders' became famous for their bravery.

Fighting in Guam and the Philippines was a different matter entirely as it involved jungle ambushes and amphibious landings, and required the complex logistics and adaptability that American forces learned the hard way. A few years later some of these troops would be involved with the great imperial powers of the world in the Boxer Rebellion in China, when they would demonstrate they were every bit the equals of their fighting counterparts from Britain, Russia and France.

The entire war lasted barely three and a half months, but it was decisive. The Spanish were crushed. However, rather than Cuba and the other possessions becoming independent, they now became American territories (for a payment to Spain of $20 million). This was empire-building – there is no other name for it, and it is a reminder that America was in no way averse to acting like the nations of Europe when it came to acquiring foreign lands.

McKinley got a taste for this by formally annexing Hawaii and the uninhabited Wake Island atoll. In the space of a handful of years, America's political and military reach had leapt from continental America into the Caribbean and across the Pacific.

The American Presidents in 100 Facts

54. WILLIAM MCKINLEY WAS THE THIRD PRESIDENT TO BE ASSASSINATED

The British Houses of Parliament and the position of Prime Minister have been around longer than America has been independent. Britain had the world's biggest empire and had fought in many international wars, so America's list of international enemies in 1901 was a lot smaller than that of Britain. Therefore it is surprising that, in a space of less than fifty years, three American presidents were assassinated, compared with just one British Prime Minister (Spencer Perceval). Indeed, in the whole of history, four American Presidents were to be assassinated compared to just the one British Prime Minister. Makes you think, doesn't it?

Shortly into his second term, the successful and popular President McKinley became the third target for assassination. Leon Frank Czolgosz (easier to write than say) was a former steelworker who had lost his job in the Panic of 1893 and had become an anarchist. McKinley's personal secretary, George Cortelyou, feared assassination attempts, especially as McKinley refused the security that was available. Cortelyou had twice postponed a presidential visit to an exposition in Buffalo, fearing McKinley would be a target, but the president loved meeting the public and twice put the visit back into his diary.

Cortelyou was right in his fears. The recent assassination of King Umberto I of Italy had galvanised the anarchists of America to plan to assassinate McKinley. Czolgosz correctly deduced that the president would be most vulnerable in a crowded area.

On 6 September 1901, McKinley finally visited the Temple of Music at the Pan-American Exposition, where he met a line of well-wishers. One of them was Czolgosz, who had hidden his pistol under a handkerchief. When Czolgosz got to the front of the line, he fired two shots into McKinley's abdomen before being wrestled to the ground. The crowd rounded furiously on Czolgosz and began to beat him savagely, when the gravely wounded McKinley shouted out, 'Boys! Don't let them hurt him!', so (temporarily) saving his assassin's life. McKinley also asked that his wife should have the news broken to her gently. These two requests from a man who had just been shot twice were the signs of a quick thinker and someone who was genuinely concerned for the welfare of others.

McKinley was rushed to hospital and over the next few days appeared to be making a recovery; however, no one knew that gangrene was slowly spreading in his stomach and fatally poisoning his blood. He died on 14 September 1901. After the murder of a third president, Congress passed legislation that charged a new body, the Secret Service, with the protection of the president.

Czolgosz was arrested and was put on trial within days. While the defence lawyers wanted more time to construct their case, it didn't help that there had been dozens of eyewitnesses and that Czolgosz did not hide the fact that he had killed the president. It took the jury only thirty minutes to come to a guilty verdict. He was convicted and executed by electric chair.

55. THEODORE ROOSEVELT WAS A SELF-MADE MAN

While some of the presidents who served terms between the times of Lincoln and Roosevelt were honourable or capable of bravery, none were giants of history. Even Grant is more famous for his service in the Civil War than for his presidency. All of this changed with Theodore Roosevelt, America's twenty-sixth president, and it is with Roosevelt that we come into the twentieth century, a time of some of America's greatest presidents, but also some of its most reviled.

At age forty-two, Roosevelt was America's youngest president and the perfect stereotype of the American outdoorsman. His vitality and bravery personified the American spirit, its 'can do' attitude ... but that's not how it started.

Unlike many other American presidents, Roosevelt was not born into poverty but into a comfortable family life in Manhattan. He was a sickly child and suffered from severe asthma, which caused debilitating night-time attacks for which no cure could be found. The boy struggled through it, forcing himself into physical fitness though his own regime of exercise.

Because of his poor health Roosevelt was taught at home by tutors, and was able to develop his love of nature by visiting the New York City zoo. When he saw a dead seal in a market, he was so fascinated that he purchased the head and learned basic taxidermy skills to preserve it. If any of this sounds made up, I promise it isn't, but a lot of Roosevelt's life reads like fiction.

Like so many of his precedents, Roosevelt went on to study law, but he found that writing his book on naval engagements was much more interesting. *The Naval War of 1812* became a bestseller, and people praised the young Roosevelt not only for his research but also for his ability to engage the reader (that's the evaluation this author is going for; you be the judge).

However, tragedy struck early in his life when his first wife died two days after giving birth to their daughter, Alice Lee Roosevelt. On the same day, his mother died of typhoid fever. Roosevelt escaped these great personal losses by taking walks in the forests and working in the New York state legislature.

While Roosevelt's political career was blossoming, his love of the American wilderness flourished. He bought land in North Dakota, learned how to ride like a cowboy, and became a deputy sheriff, successfully hunting down a band of thieves.

In December of 1886, he remarried to Edith Kermit Carow, a childhood friend. They travelled to Europe on their honeymoon and climbed Mont Blanc together because ... well ... it was Roosevelt. They went on to have five children.

Roosevelt became the New York City Police Commissioner and was described as 'an iron-willed leader of unimpeachable honesty'. A few years later McKinley made Roosevelt the Assistant Secretary of the Navy, but that didn't stop him giving up the desk job and fighting in Cuba (Fact 53). This unstoppable man of action fought in his first war at the age of forty.

56. Roosevelt Was Accidentally a Great President

McKinley's first vice president was Garret Hobart. He and McKinley worked well together, and Roosevelt would have been able to spend the rest of his years being larger-than-life in places other than the White House had Hobart not suddenly died of heart failure in 1899. McKinley did not have a vice president for the rest of his first term. However, for his second term McKinley chose as his running mate the politically inexperienced Roosevelt, mainly because of his popularity as a war hero. After four years as vice president, and after the lustre of his war record would have faded, whether Roosevelt would have been the Republicans' first choice is a matter of conjecture, but an assassin's bullet made that a moot point, and two unforeseen deaths meant that Roosevelt was now the President of the United States.

Once this spirited man took office, it was anyone's guess what his policies would be. He had echoes of Grant: both were war heroes who as presidents preferred the peaceful option almost every time. For example, during a coal strike in 1902, Roosevelt managed to negotiate a settlement when other presidents had sent in troops to break things up. He described his foreign policy as 'speak softly and carry a big stick'.

As a man who had grown up in a wealthy family, it seemed counter-intuitive for Roosevelt to go after powerful big business, but his administration became known for his anti-monopoly policies. The monopolies were known as trusts, and Roosevelt raised so much legislation to break their power that he got the nickname 'trust buster'.

Roosevelt was a nature lover and recognised the value of preserving the countryside. America owes nearly 200 million acres of national forest and parkland to his foresight. Some of this legacy can be seen from Mount Rushmore, where Roosevelt's face is one of the four carved into the rock (for more on this see Fact 66).

Inspired by the Suez Canal, he was a great advocate of the Panama Canal to improve maritime access and trade in the Americas. The project turned out to be more complex than anyone had imagined and was not completed until after Roosevelt's presidency.

Finally, as an ardent imperialist and a man who never backed down from a fight, it is surprising to discover that Roosevelt was awarded the Noble Peace Prize. Russia and Japan had the first major international conflict of the twentieth century, and the world was shocked when, for the first time, an Asian power beat a European one. It was Roosevelt, however, who brokered the peace terms between Tsarist Russia and Imperial Japan. The talks culminated in the Treaty of Portsmouth, and peace was secured. Roosevelt used his money from the Nobel Prize to fund a trust to promote industrial peace.

For a man who shouldn't have been president, Roosevelt astonished everyone with his considered and effective leadership. Therefore it came as no surprise that when he ran for re-election in 1904, he crushed the Democratic candidate, Alton B. Parker, at the polls.

57. Roosevelt Kept Himself Busy Even after His Presidency

If there is one word to describe Roosevelt it would be 'restless'. It is rare to come across a person in history who was effective in politics, wrote numerous books and was also a man of adventure, having fought in war and remained willing to do so again.

However, there needs to be balance, and Roosevelt was not a flawless human being. While he was the first president to appoint a Jew to the Cabinet, he made some highly disparaging remarks about Native Americans and only tolerated African Americans. That said, he did appoint multiple African Americans to federal offices.

Roosevelt was also the quintessential 'great white hunter'. He went to Africa and killed almost every species of big game. Many were preserved and sent to the Smithsonian Institution for scientific study and public display, but today's readers would be uneasy seeing pictures of Roosevelt holding a rifle, standing proudly next to an elephant he had shot. However, his journeys to Africa and, later, South America led to more books (some twenty-five, on a range of subjects) and popular lectures at the National Geographic Museum.

The reality is that Roosevelt was the quintessential Victorian man-of-action, like Frederick Selous, Robert Baden-Powell or Adrian Carton de Wiart (for more on Selous and de Wiart, see my book *Forgotten History*). These were all brave men with remarkable stories, but when their actions or comments are taken out of the context of their times, some things to modern sensibilities look like racism. Roosevelt's best characteristics are timeless; his worst are the trappings of the Victorian age.

During a hunting trip in Mississippi in 1902, Roosevelt refused to shoot a black bear tied to a tree. A cartoon of the incident was published in the *Washington Post* and a toy maker subsequently produced a stuffed bear which he called the 'Teddy Bear', named after Roosevelt. The nickname stuck for both man and bear.

In 1912 Roosevelt came out of retirement to run for president again, this time as the candidate of his own Progressive Party. He came second to Woodrow Wilson but comprehensively beat his old Republican party. That wasn't the only excitement in 1912, as another lone gunman tried to kill the ex-president. However the bullet was slowed as it passed through a metal case and folded speech in Roosevelt's pocket, allowing him to survive and make a full recovery.

When the First World War broke out in 1914, Roosevelt enlisted to lead American forces. He was a staunch supporter of the Allies against Germany, but America was not to enter the war until 1917; although Roosevelt didn't serve, one of his sons died in a fighter plane on the Western Front in 1918. Roosevelt fell ill in January of 1919 and, most unexpectedly, died in his sleep at the age of sixty. His son Archibald telegraphed news to the family, stating bluntly but somewhat poetically, 'The old lion is dead.'

Theodore Roosevelt was the first president to be awarded the Medal of Honor, posthumously, by President Bill Clinton.

58. William Howard Taft Was a Smart Man but an Average President

After all the excitement that swirled around Teddy Roosevelt, it's hard to see William Howard Taft, America's twenty-seventh president, as anything other than an anti-climax. Taft was Roosevelt's hand-picked successor and his credentials were impeccable.

Taft was yet another lawyer who was lured to politics. He was born into a prominent and ambitious family in Ohio, and his father had big plans for him. When Taft graduated 'only' second in his Yale law class, his father was deeply disappointed.

Taft began his legal career as an assistant prosecutor in his home state and became a judge in his twenties. It was about this time that he met his wife Helen (known as Nellie). They had three children and were said to have had a happy marriage, although Nellie was no shy violet and pushed Taft as hard as his parents had done – and that's saying something. Taft's long-term personal ambition was to become a Supreme Court Justice, but Nellie and the family had plans that meant pursuing a political career.

In 1890, after narrowly missing out on a place in the Supreme Court, Taft was appointed United States Solicitor General which, for those of you who aren't up on your judicial hierarchy, is the third highest ranking official in the US Department of Justice. This was impressive considering he was just thirty-two at the time.

In 1901, President McKinley made him the first civilian Governor of the Philippines. It was thought that the fair and honest Taft could calm a simmering rebellion for independence that was threatening the country. Taft did the best job possible under the circumstances, even appealing to the Pope to help calm the situation in the Catholic Philippines. That didn't work, but he left the island nation in a better state than he had found it.

From 1904 to 1908, Taft was Roosevelt's Secretary of War. Despite the title, he used the position to negotiate peacefully with Japan to protect the Philippines, a country for which he had developed a soft spot. Unlike most of the Americans who administered the islands, Taft treated the Filipinos as social equals and believed that the US should work in partnership with the people. To that end he supported legislation that allowed Filipino agricultural produce to enter the US mainland tariff free. This boosted their economy and gave the Filipinos a reason to work with America.

With his track record and Roosevelt's backing, Taft won the 1908 election by a landslide; however, his four years as president were marked by a lot of talking and not much action. Taft didn't destroy the economy or take the country into war, but neither did the economy boom and nor were there any military victories or major pieces of legislation. He was the presidential equivalent of a caretaker. When the next election came, the Republican vote was split by Roosevelt returning to the race with his new Progressive Party. Taft came a distant third, with the Democrats reaping the benefits of the split.

59. TAFT HAD AN EMBARRASSING PRIVATE LIFE

The previous fact shows that President Taft was an honest and principled individual, but that's not what people remember about him. William Howard Taft was the fattest president ever. How fat? He ordered a new and much larger bath (to fit four men) for the White House after he (allegedly) got stuck in the old one.

But this was not his only source of embarrassment. His fiery wife Nellie took things to a whole new level when, in 1912, she turned up at the Democratic National Congress and sat in a front-row seat to intimidate Democratic hopefuls into toning down their personal attacks on her Republican husband. It worked. (It is worth noting that this happened before women had the vote in America.)

Finally, Taft marked the end of an era. After all the beards, moustaches and sideburns of the past, Taft was the last president to have facial hair.

Free of the presidency, Taft lost seventy pounds. How did he do this? He cut carbohydrates and alcohol from his diet and said afterwards, 'Too much flesh is bad for any man.'

Taft served as a Professor of Law at Yale University until President Harding made him Chief Justice of the United States Supreme Court in 1921. He held the position until just before his death in 1930 at the age of seventy-two. The appointment was the fulfilment of a lifelong dream. It is clear what it meant to him when he wrote, 'I don't remember that I ever was president.'

60. WOODROW WILSON WAS A PRESIDENT IN A HURRY

In 1912 the Democrats scored two critical victories: they gained a majority in Congress and Woodrow Wilson won the presidential election to become the twenty-eighth President of the United States. Wilson had both a mandate to govern and the majority in Congress to do something about it.

The checks and balances created by the Founding Fathers to protect the government from the rise of tyranny have the real world problem that it can be difficult for a president to get anything done. If Congress (composed of the House of Representatives and the Senate) and the president are not of the same party, the president needs to do a lot of negotiating and compromising to get legislation passed. By and large the system worked until the end of the twentieth century, when parties in opposition to the president have used their power to block his proposals. With all of this in mind, Wilson's position could not have been bettered, and he had a greater chance to enact legislation than most other presidents. He once said:

> The government, which was designed for the people, has got into the hands of the bosses and their employers, the special interests. An invisible empire has been set up above the forms of democracy.

But then he also said:

> The only use of an obstacle is to be overcome. All that an obstacle does with brave men is, not to frighten them, but to challenge them.

Wilson's actions demonstrated that he clearly believed in both quotes. During his eight years in office, Congress passed two constitutional amendments: the prohibition of alcohol (Eighteenth) and women's suffrage (Nineteenth). The former had the strong, vocal support of the Woman's Christian Temperance Union (WCTU), but Wilson believed it to be unenforceable. He vetoed its passage and it was Congress which passed it over the president's veto. Two other far-reaching amendments were ratified while Wilson was president: the Sixteenth allows Congress to levy income tax and introduced the concept of graduated tax; the Seventeenth provides for the direct election of Senators.

Under his presidency Congress passed the Clayton Antitrust Act, a piece of legislation designed to tackle anti-competitive practices. It was a giant leap forward in 'trust buster' legislation.

When the Colorado miners went on strike in 1914, Wilson sent in the National Guard, which led to the Ludlow Massacre. Eighteen people died – eleven of them children. The massacre so shocked America it led to a standard eight-hour workday and substantial changes to child labour laws.

In the same year Wilson's wife died of kidney failure. It took Wilson time to recover, but he soon fell in love with Edith Galt. Unfazed by the attentions of the US President, Edith rebuffed his advances, but Wilson continued to pursue her: they married in December of 1915. Wilson was then in his late fifties; Edith was in her early forties. They had no children (he had three daughters by his first wife) but remained together until Wilson's death nine years later.

THE AMERICAN PRESIDENTS IN 100 FACTS

61. America Took Most of The First World War to Join In

The threat of war hung over Europe in the summer of 1914, and everyone, including America, could see that a titanic clash of empires was inevitable. Roosevelt was staunchly on the side of France and Britain, two democracies going up against the German Kaiser's dictatorship. This story became even more compelling after Germany invaded Belgium, France and areas of the Russian Empire. Wilson did not agree with Roosevelt, who had enlisted and was ready to fight, so America stood on the side lines as the Western Front fossilised into the deadly trench warfare which would become the defining image of that war.

Instead, Wilson took a different tact, moulding America as the potential broker of peace. Regarding America's stance to the war, he spoke of its 'true spirit of neutrality, which is the spirit of impartiality and fairness and friendliness to all concerned'.

In a way Wilson was following Roosevelt's own career. Had Roosevelt not won a Noble Peace Prize for brokering peace between Russia and Japan? It is also worth saying that millions were dying in Europe, and, while the European powers had everything to fight for, what would America gain if it sent hundreds of thousands of its young men to their deaths? It didn't seem a politically astute or morally correct position for America to go to war.

Britain blockaded neutral shipping (including American vessels) from docking in Germany. Technically, this was an act of war, and, technically, similar British maritime actions had triggered the War of 1812, but Wilson argued that this was a mild inconvenience to remain on the edge of the conflict. By contrast, however, Germany declared unrestricted submarine warfare, effectively making the Atlantic Ocean a new front, where nobody was neutral. This was to result in the infamous sinking of the *Lusitania* in 1915. More than a thousand passengers died, hundreds of them American, but it was an outrage that has been misremembered as the trigger for America's declaration of war on Germany. America remonstrated loudly against Germany, and Americans of German ancestry were horrified (the author's own family dropped the second 'n' in a German surname to sound less German), but war was not declared. 1915 also saw other (probably accidental) attacks on American ships by the German navy.

Wilson won a landslide victory in the 1916 election with the slogan, 'He kept us out of the war,' which is not the same thing as 'He won't go to war,' but the message was clear that America largely agreed with Wilson. It wasn't until early 1917 that Wilson eventually joined the Allied side. The straw that broke the camel's back was a deciphered secret telegram from Germany to Mexico encouraging Mexico to invade Texas. It was a clear act of war, so brazen that Wilson initially thought it was a British forgery (for more on the Zimmermann telegram read *The British Empire in 100 Facts*). Finally, on 4 April 1917, an official declaration of war was passed by strong bipartisan majorities.

62. AMERICA FOUGHT TO THE END OF THE FIRST WORLD WAR

After years of avoiding war, Wilson now had to prepare the country to fight in Europe. By the winter of 1918 America had mobilized around 4 million military personnel and, by the Armistice in November 1918, had suffered around 110,000 dead. Almost a third of those were from the lethal influenza pandemic which travelled the world in the winter of 1918/19.

For Britain and France, America's involvement came at a critical time: Russia had just been knocked out of the war by the revolution going on at home. This freed up more than a million German soldiers from the Eastern Front, enabling them to be deployed elsewhere.

As most people know, the front lines in this war rapidly solidified. This meant few major changes to the areas of conflict, and it soon became a war of attrition. America had missed the epic battles of Verdun and the Somme, where millions had fought and hundreds of thousands had died. All sides were simply running out of men, but with a fresh injection of millions of American troops in the summer of 1918, Germany either had to win quickly or lose due to lack of numbers. The Germans threw everything they had left into their spring offensive. The Anglo-French front lines buckled but didn't break. After that, more and more American soldiers were arriving to reinforce the Allied front line.

At first the Americans failed to listen to their allies and made all the (now avoidable) mistakes Britain and France had made at the start of the war. Thousands died needlessly as hard-won lessons were learned. The harsh reality was that, in a way, America could afford to make mistakes: on average, 10,000 American soldiers were arriving in mainland Europe every day.

However, while America fought for less than a year, with far less blood spilled than any other of the Allies, it was a major force at the end of the war. Wilson played a significant role in the Paris peace talks and returned home with the Versailles Treaty, which included a proposal for an international body called the League of Nations (the forerunner of the United Nations). Wilson's party had lost its majority in the 1918 election; the Republicans now had the numbers, and ratification of the treaty failed by seven votes. In the end America negotiated its own peace terms with Germany and its allies.

In the winter of 1918, Russia was still embroiled in a vicious civil war, while Britain and France had their mighty empires. America was still a second-rate power by comparison, but the First World War was a sign of things to come. The Europeans might then have been much more powerful, but their time was coming to an end.

The idea of an association of nations originated with Wilson, who first mentioned it in a speech to Congress in January of 1918, but when the European powers created the League of Nations, the Americans were nowhere to be seen. Politics forced Wilson to decline to join.

63. THE 1920 PRESIDENTIAL ELECTION WAS AN ANTI-CLIMAX

By 1920 Woodrow Wilson had become one of the most successful presidents in a century. He had given women the vote, first avoided and then fought in a worldwide conflict – on the winning side – and raised the global standing of America. True, there had been riots and industrial disputes which were hotly contested at the time, but in the long term America was better off and more secure after Wilson's presidency than before it. Therefore, it was with a palpable sense of disappointment that he didn't run for a third term. Nobody was surprised. Towards the end of his second term he had suffered a severe stroke and barely recovered, but he would have been in a very strong position to win a third term.

After the usual selection process, the Democrats chose James Cox, Governor of Ohio. Cox was intelligent, well-connected and a good public speaker. He even had an eye for potential as his choice of vice presidential running mate was the young but promising Franklin D. Roosevelt (Teddy's fifth cousin). Cox was running against the Republican Senator, and newspaper publisher, Warren Harding, who had Calvin Coolidge as his running mate. This is an interesting snapshot in time, as all of these men – except for Cox – would go on to become president.

For better or worse, none of these men were 'big names', a factor that would influence the election turnout, if not the results themselves. After his Progressive Party failed, the Republicans seriously considered bringing back Teddy Roosevelt as their candidate, but Roosevelt's rapidly declining health put an end to that.

On paper Cox was the better candidate and played well with Americans of both Irish and German descent, but Harding made the better argument. Harding played on the war weariness of the general public; his talk of a return to 'normalcy' held great appeal at the end of a major conflict.

The 1920 election was particularly important because it was the first since the Nineteenth Amendment to the Constitution gave women in every state the right to vote. This led to a huge but not unexpected jump in the number of registered voters (18.5 million in 1916 compared to 26.8 million in 1920). While Cox and Franklin Roosevelt were energetic in their campaigning (something that would be remembered about Roosevelt in later years), Cox was to suffer the most crushing defeat in American electoral history. Harding received a shade over 60 per cent of the popular vote and carried thirty-seven states to Cox's eleven.

Another interesting point about this election was the decrease in the name recognition of the presidential candidates. Despite women now being able to vote, failure to recognise the candidates led to one of the lowest voter turnouts in American history at around 49 per cent of the registered voters (in 1916 it was 61.6 per cent). However, low voter turnout or not, Warren Harding was inaugurated as the twenty-ninth president in March of 1921.

64. Warren G. Harding Was a Popular but Scandalous President

Warren Harding was a much-loved president. He oversaw the return of economic growth after a recent recession, and he was seen as an accomplished statesman.

In some respects Harding was ahead of his time in urging equal political rights for African Americans. Unfortunately, it was a sign of the times that Harding had to bring in anti-lynching laws to protect these same African Americans. He pardoned a number of political prisoners, including Eugene Debs, a cause célèbre who had been sentenced to ten years in prison for speaking out against American involvement in the First World War. Also on the domestic front, Harding signed the Federal Highways Act under which the government spent $162 million on America's highway system in 1921-3. This boosted employment and provided a much-needed infrastructure for the country's growing economy.

Internationally, Harding did well too. He was the president who formally signed all the peace treaties to end America's involvement in the First World War. He also kept the new Soviet Union at arm's length, recognising it as a political opponent to American ideals. Harding pledged to reduce American military interventions in South America and removed US troops from Cuba.

All these policies (and more) made him a tremendously popular president. But then Harding died unexpectedly in August of 1923. He had been on a cross-country tour when he became ill and died from heart failure in a San Francisco hotel. No autopsy was carried out, which led to unfounded rumours that his wife had smothered him with a pillow when she discovered that he was having an extramarital affair. The affair was real, but he died of congenital heart failure, not asphyxiation.

While Harding had made many capable appointments to his Cabinet (Herbert Hoover, a future president, was Secretary of Commerce), he allowed himself to be surrounded by dubious characters who were later found to be guilty of criminal activities. Prior to his trip, Harding had asked Hoover how best to handle the storm of scandal he saw coming. Hoover advised him to go public, but Harding was worried about the political fallout. In the event, a tidal wave of scandal came crashing down on the deceased president's legacy. The most infamous was the Teapot Dome scandal in which his Secretary of the Interior, Albert Fall, took bribes in return for leasing lands with untapped oil reserves to private companies (Teapot Dome in Wyoming was one such example). Fall was the only member of the Cabinet ever to go to prison. Many other government officials were found to be guilty of taking bribes or embezzling government funds.

Harding himself was never accused of criminal activity, but the allegations of extramarital affairs and alcohol in the White House (during the era of Prohibition) were, without the scandals and corruption, enough to have ensured that he could never have won a second term. It's also entirely possible that he would have been impeached. His death occurred at exactly the right time for Harding to miss the storms he had seen coming.

65. CALVIN COOLIDGE WAS KNOWN AS 'SILENT CAL'

A total of eight US Presidents have died in office (four by assassination). At 19 per cent, that's a higher mortality rate than that of a US combat soldier in the Second World War. It seems that being President of the United States is, statistically, one of the most lethal jobs in the world. With Harding's sudden death, a vice president, once again, became the new president.

Calvin Coolidge, America's thirtieth president, stepped into his role just as all the scandals from Harding's presidency were becoming common knowledge. In that atmosphere, there was every reason to think that Coolidge himself might become mired in all the corruption. However, Coolidge had a secret weapon: he was dull. A common characteristic of dull people is that they are honest – and to be fair to Coolidge, he could deliver a good speech from time to time. But the president was notoriously quiet at social gatherings, preferring instead that his loquacious wife be the life and soul of the party. This led to his nickname 'Silent Cal'.

One of the best-known stories about him (although it could be apocryphal) concerns a comment he made while attending a dinner party with his wife. The woman sitting next to Coolidge, attempting to engage him in conversation, allegedly said, 'I made a bet today that I could get more than two words out of you.' Coolidge retorted with, 'You lose.' He then got up and left.

True or not, it was an indication of his taciturn nature that this story was widely believed. Coolidge, in his own limited words, said:

> The words of a President have an enormous weight ... and ought not to be used indiscriminately.

Although not of the archetypal log cabin origin, Coolidge came from a humble background, and his plainness and honesty appealed to broad swathes of the electorate. Coolidge was also a moral and religious man who continued Harding's policies (the good ones) and retained his entire Cabinet as that was what the people of America had voted for in 1920. Coolidge also made the valid point that people are innocent until proven guilty and gave the benefit of the doubt to any of the Cabinet members associated with scandal.

However, this is not to say that he didn't want to root out corruption. He regarded it as an honour and a privilege to be America's president, and he was determined to treat the position with the respect it deserved. Coolidge used his presidential veto and pardon extensively, allowing himself to carve the role of president in the image he had in mind. Therefore, after the fallout from Harding's presidency, Coolidge emerged from the quagmire unblemished. At the time of his inauguration, it looked like he would be in office only until the next election in 1924, but by then he was so admired that the Republicans selected him as their candidate. He ran against the Democrat John Davis and the (revived) Progressive Party's Robert La Follette Sr. Coolidge won by a landslide.

66. PRESIDENTS ROCK

South Dakota had a problem: nobody wanted to go there. It doesn't have any wonders of nature, like the Grand Canyon; it isn't the site of any notable battles; it doesn't have the attractions of a big city like New York. Doane Robinson, a state historian, took the decision to do something to put South Dakota on the map. He conceived a plan to carve giant likenesses of the four most popular presidents into a cliff face. Mr Robinson came up with the idea for the Mount Rushmore National Memorial.

A delegation from South Dakota visited President Coolidge (renowned for his advocacy of small government) who, somewhat surprisingly, bought into the idea of spending taxpayers' money on a colossal monument with no discernible purpose (other than tourism).

In some ways Mount Rushmore is the perfect metaphor for America and its presidents. It is truly impressive and stands as a symbol of the civic pride Americans have in their greatest presidents. It is also the physical embodiment of man's triumph over nature, as these sculptures are hewn from granite, one of the hardest rocks. However, it is not what was originally planned – which was a poorly conceived project with little consideration for Native American traditions.

Let's break things down. The original intention was to sculpt images of the presidents from head to waist, but the money ran out, so the visitor today just gets heads (plus a little more of Washington). There had also been plans for key documents to be carved into the mountain. The Declaration of Independence was to be memorialised in eight-foot-tall gilded letters, but that never happened. Also, the order of the presidents on the monument is odd. It goes (left to right): George

Washington, Thomas Jefferson, Theodore Roosevelt and Abraham Lincoln. Except that this is not the order of their presidencies, nor is it their order in terms of popularity or importance. It seems to be a bizarrely haphazard arrangement.

The next issue was that of the mountain itself. Known to Native Americans as the 'Six Grandfathers', Mount Rushmore is a spiritual site and an area of historic significance to the Lakota Sioux, whose leader, Black Elk, had a spiritual experience there. Therefore, the complete remoulding of the area for nothing nobler than the pursuit of tourist dollars is an emblem of US governmental ambivalence (or worse) towards Native American culture.

Gutzon Borglum began work on the site in 1927 and took more than a decade to chisel out the sixty-foot-high faces. The project came to an end in 1941 when the money ran out. The elaborate plan had not been completed, but by then the government had more pressing priorities in waging the Second World War.

The site has been developed over the decades, with a large visitor centre added in 1998. On average the park receives over 3 million visitors annually. This means that when Doane Robinson's original (and slightly crazy) plan to put South Dakota on the tourist trail was finally realised, it was a great success.

67. Calvin Coolidge Was Popular because He Was Bland

After the 1924 election Coolidge felt he had a mandate to eject most of Harding's old Cabinet, and his policies, while always leaning towards 'small government', were not newsworthy. In Calvin Coolidge's America the economy ticked along and the government had a budget surplus (an enviable record).

By the time of his presidency, the Eighteenth Amendment (passed in 1920), which outlawed the manufacture, transport and sale of alcohol, had been in place for a few years, and the 'Roaring Twenties' were in full swing. The amendment was unenforceable and cities like Chicago were overrun by organised bootlegging (the illegal production of alcohol) and racketeering, as well as gang warfare. This was the era of Al Capone and George 'Bugs' Moran. Yet despite all this seedy glamour and violence, the country was led by a calm and considered individual. So when it came to the 1928 election, everyone expected Coolidge to run again. However in 1927, while on vacation near Mount Rushmore (see previous fact; at this time still under construction), he gathered the press and announced, in his usual blunt manner, that he wouldn't be running again.

He later explained he had had enough; he was tired. As it happened, he would not have survived to the end of a third term as he died in January of 1933. When he was asked to endorse the next Republican candidate, Herbert Hoover, Coolidge declined, saying, 'For six years that man has given me unsolicited advice—all of it bad.'

68. HERBERT HOOVER WAS AN UNLUCKY PRESIDENT

Unlike most of his predecessors who chose one of the three popular routes to the job, Hoover was not a military man, a lawyer or a career politician (better if it was two out of three). Although he had spent more than a decade in Washington before getting involved in politics, Hoover came from an engineering background. To say that he was an unusual candidate for president would be an understatement, but in the presidential election of 1928, he easily won against the Democrat Al Smith to become the 31st President of the United States. And, surprisingly, after the record low turnouts of the previous two elections, a significant number of voters returned for this one.

However, no one could have known that Hoover was inheriting a poisoned chalice. Eight months after he took office, the American stock market crashed in October of 1929. This sent the economy into a decade-long tailspin, which took two different presidencies to resolve. Because the disaster had been stored up in the previous presidency, Hoover, in theory, could avoid blame, but with the Republicans having won three terms in a row, economic mismanagement was squarely at the door of the Republican Party rather than the Democrats.

It has been misremembered that Hoover did little to try and alleviate the situation. The reality was that Franklin Roosevelt's New Deal, which was an ambitious plan to spend federal money to increase jobs and demand, started under Hoover. Hoover spent over $1.5 billion on various governmental projects from shipping, to farm subsidies, to colossal projects like the Hoover Dam (and, of course, Mount Rushmore continued to get funding during this time).

However, even with massive injections of government money, Hoover was fighting against a tide of a global recession. Britain managed to avoid the worst extremes of the crisis thanks to the trade agreements within its empire (the world's largest ever empire was then at its peak). Germany was facing its second major economic crisis in a decade, an economic instability that would lead to the eventual election of Hitler as chancellor. With an economic hurricane roaring across the globe, no one country could simply spend its way back into growth.

When people failed to keep up with rent or mortgage payments, they became homeless. Shanty towns grew up from nowhere – many were bitterly called 'Hooverville'. There was even a Hooverville in Central Park in New York City. A 'Hoover Wagon' was a car or truck pulled by horses because the owner either couldn't afford to repair the vehicle or couldn't afford the fuel.

President Hoover became the face of economic failure, but he worried that any new Republican candidate in 1932 would come up with some kind of radical measure to fix the economy. Therefore, even though he had grown tired of being president, and he must have known it was inevitable that he would lose, he ran in 1932 against Franklin D. Roosevelt. Herbert Hoover, a moral man, was in the wrong place at the wrong time.

69. THE 1932 PRESIDENTIAL ELECTION WAS ABOUT BEER AND MONEY

The author of this book has held a minor elected office, and it is my experience that, while those in authority think that the man in the street really cares about immigration or foreign policy, what he really cares about are the things that immediately affect him. For example, if a person is anti-immigration but really wants the road resurfaced, he doesn't enquire about the nationality of the workmen who resurface the road. He's just happy the road is fixed.

Good political campaigns tap into this truth and, rather than talk about high level political concepts, try to make a difference to the lives of voters. In 1932 Franklin Roosevelt fought one of the most basic and populist campaigns in American history. He chose as his campaign song 'Happy Days Are Here Again', a catchy tune with an unambiguous message. It was during the presidency of the Democrat Woodrow Wilson that alcohol had been banned, but by 1932 it was the Republicans who defended the ban while the Democrats sensed that the country had had enough. Like Prohibition, the Great Depression had rumbled on for years, so Roosevelt laid all the blame he could on Herbert Hoover and the Republican Party.

Hoover had been the president when the country fell off a cliff, and he was left with a divided party and little in the way of a populist message. The results were a landslide for Roosevelt, who won forty-two of the forty-eight states.

70. IN 1933 AMERICA GOT A NEW DEAL

Franklin Delano Roosevelt, known as FDR, was America's thirty-second president, and one of the few who not only fulfilled his electoral pledges, but continued the spirit of his campaign into his presidency. More than anything else, Roosevelt was a showman. It was in his first inaugural speech that he declared, 'The only thing we have to fear is fear itself.'

In 1933 he created 'The New Deal', the cornerstone of which was relief for the poor and unemployed, economic recovery, and reform of the financial system to prevent a repeat of the panic of 1929. All of this was sensible stuff – so sensible that it was exactly what Hoover had been doing before the election.

So why did it work under Roosevelt and not Hoover? The answer is simple: four years after the stock market crash, the world's economy was starting to recover. Roosevelt was swimming with the prevailing economic current, not against it as Hoover had been doing. Even though for the first few years of his presidency the economy had yet to return to pre-Depression levels (and unemployment was still high), the perception was that Roosevelt was fixing the nation. We are back to the observation in the previous fact that leaders need to make a difference to individual voters. Roosevelt got lucky by doing the same thing his predecessor had done, but this time it not only worked but was seen to work – more by fortuitous timing than anything else.

Going back a few elections, a year after he campaigned in 1920, Roosevelt fell ill and was diagnosed with polio, which left him paralysed from the waist down. He refused to accept that he was permanently paralysed and underwent a wide range of therapies. He also managed to convince others that he was on the road to recovery, even going so far as to walk short distances while wearing iron braces. There are 125,000 photos of Roosevelt in the FDR presidential library, and only two show him in a wheelchair. Roosevelt understood that image is vital in politics, and as such he could not be seen as physically weak, even if that meant projecting a distorted image.

Roosevelt liked 'good news' stories and to this end made Frances Perkins a member of his Cabinet. She was his Secretary of Labor, the first woman to hold a Cabinet post, which was a major leap forward for women who, just fifteen years earlier, didn't even have the right to vote. This played well with female voters and boosted Roosevelt's popularity, which would later help his chances for re-election.

Also in the 'good news' category was the fulfilment of the promise to America that adults could, once again, enjoy a beer. Roosevelt signed the Cullen–Harrison Act in March 1933, which paved the way for the Twenty-first Amendment to the Constitution. This repealed Prohibition and was ratified by the end of the same year. Presumably everyone but the bootleggers and the Woman's Christian Temperance Union celebrated with a drink.

As the economy improved and an air of optimism returned, FDR was always going to be the favourite going into the 1936 election. The Republicans settled on Alf Landon, and if you've never heard of him, he wasn't that well-known in America either. His campaign was lacklustre, to say the least. In one period during the campaign, he made no speeches for two months. Democracy demands a choice of candidate, but this candidate really didn't have his heart in the race.

The result was a foregone conclusion. Come the election year, Roosevelt was wildly popular. In another landslide victory he once again won forty-six of the forty-eight states. It wasn't just good news for Roosevelt, but for the Democratic Party as a whole: the so-called 'New Deal Democrats' won even larger majorities in Congress. FDR had a mandate to continue to mould the country his way, much to the chagrin of the Republicans.

Roosevelt's second term would continue to be dominated by the economy, which was improving all the time; but behind the silver lining, the storm clouds of war were gathering. Roosevelt always had a good instinct for what the public wanted, and he knew that America was isolationist in its approach to the wider world. As evil as Hitler was, it simply wasn't perceived as America's war ... yet.

After the Supreme Court overturned many of his pet programs, FDR became preoccupied with the workings of the court and, in 1937, stunned Congress by proposing a law to allow him to appoint up to six new justices. This was seen as a step too far even by his own party, and it failed to get any serious traction. But time was on Roosevelt's side, and he was able to appoint new justices as the older ones died off, one by one. By 1941, Roosevelt had appointed seven of the nine justices, which, unsurprisingly, resulted in the court ratifying his policies.

The 1940 election went a little better for the Republicans and their candidate, Wendell Willkie. This was the election when the Second World War was raging across Europe and Africa, and Roosevelt declared that there would be no involvement in foreign wars if he were re-elected (his hand would be forced just over a year later). This time around he only won thirty-eight of the forty-eight states – still an enviable achievement.

In 1944 Roosevelt was re-elected for a fourth time. On this occasion the Republican candidate, Thomas Dewey, managed to win twelve states, which was not bad considering, that by then America was in the midst of a global war.

Roosevelt's election to a record fourth term was to become a unique moment in US history. FDR died early in 1945, which led Congress to propose, and in 1951 to ratify, the Twenty-second Amendment to the Constitution. This limited future presidents to two terms only. This meant that, since no one can now win more than two elections, FDR will always be the longest-serving president in US history.

72. Roosevelt Led America into The Second World War

During the 1940 campaign Roosevelt said that he did not want to fight in foreign wars. All that changed on 7 December 1941. Without declaring war on America, Imperial Japan attacked the US naval base at Pearl Harbor in Hawaii. It was the most devastating sneak attack by another country in history: nearly 2,500 people died and key parts of America's Pacific fleet were destroyed.

The original draft of FDR's Pearl Harbor speech contained the phrase 'a day that will live in world history'. Roosevelt personally amended it to 'a day that will live in infamy'.

No country could fail to respond to such an attack, and America had an obvious target in Japan, an Axis ally. But FDR recognised that, once America was involved in the war, it was the Nazi regime in Europe which posed the bigger threat. How could FDR convince America (many Americans had German ancestry) to fight again in Europe? The answer came just a few days later when, conveniently for FDR (and the Allies), Hitler declared war on America.

By the time America was finally mobilising and getting involved in a fight that had been raging for years, it was 1942. Logic would dictate that America should have thrown its weight at Japan; instead, it first poured men and resources into helping Europe dismantle the Nazi war machine. This was one of the reasons why the Pacific campaign lasted longer than the European one.

Putting aside technological developments, the major strategic difference between the situation when America joined the fight in the First World War and that when it joined the Second World War was the role of the Soviet Union. In 1918 the Allies had desperately needed the injection of fresh American troops when Russia withdrew from the conflict, but come the Second World War Russia, now the Soviet Union, was very much involved in the struggle on the Eastern Front. The confrontation between Axis forces and those of the Soviets was one of the largest and bloodiest battles in history. From Hitler's perspective, by 1944 two-thirds of his forces were fighting in the East, with the other third fighting both Britain and America. It was inevitable that Germany would lose to three colossal armies.

The fight in the Pacific ended when America dropped two nuclear bombs on mainland Japan. The task of developing such revolutionary weapons (the Manhattan Project) is the single most expensive project in human history. The moral arguments rumble on.

If the war introduced American military might to the world, it also introduced American culture. Wherever they were, American troops wanted home comforts and familiar goods, so Coca-Cola was tasked with setting up new factories to meet the demand and inadvertently turned itself into a global brand. The culture spread further with the Marshall Plan, in which American money was used to rebuild Europe, including Britain. It was the Second World War that made America the superpower it continues to be today – and yet it was a war America did not want to fight.

73. HARRY S. TRUMAN WAS THE THIRTY-THIRD PRESIDENT

After winning an historic fourth term, FDR died in April of 1945. America was shocked. Hitler, however, saw it as an opportunity, hoping this would temporarily knock America out of the war, but Hitler was wrong (and not just about this). The United States had lost presidents before, and Vice President Harry S. Truman was a decisive man.

In fact there was only one indecisive thing about Truman: his middle name or, rather, the lack thereof. His parents couldn't decide on a middle name, so they simply went with the letter 'S' on the birth certificate, to honour both of his grandparents, Shippe and Solomon. The omission became an issue during his first inauguration when Chief Justice Harlan Stone said, 'I, Harry Shippe Truman ...' and Truman replied, 'I, Harry S. Truman ...', gently correcting the chief justice.

By the time Truman became president, the war in Europe was in its death throes. There was little left for him to do, and within a month it was over. There was still, however, hard fighting to be done in the Pacific. Truman had to make a number of incredibly tough decisions over the course of his presidency, but the hardest was the first: whether to drop nuclear bombs on Japan.

This moral dilemma could compose a book in itself. So let's look first at the arguments against: tens of thousands of civilians would die. A negotiated peace (rather than an unconditional surrender) could be proposed. A conventional invasion could be carried out on the home islands of Japan (assuming the Americans would win in a land invasion).

The arguments in favour: first of all, there was no appetite for a negotiated surrender, not after the unprovoked attack on Pearl Harbor and the viciousness of the fighting that followed. Second, while civilians would die, how many more American troops would perish in any fight to invade and conquer Japan? Battles on Okinawa showed that Japanese soldiers were willing to fight to the last man and that many civilians would rather commit suicide than suffer the humiliation of capture. There was no evidence to suggest that the Japanese would ever agree to a negotiated peace. The plan for an invasion of Honshu anticipated huge numbers of casualties (it also, with hindsight, underestimated the number of kamikaze fighters ready to attack).

If the loss of human life is 'bad', then the option where the fewest people die is the least bad option. That was Truman's basic reasoning, and, while counter-factual history is notoriously full of supposition, and while it would be nice to think that there was a solution that didn't involve significant loss of life, this author doesn't believe that, in 1945, there was one.

It is also worth remembering that the Japanese did not surrender after Hiroshima. Admiral Toyoda even said, 'There may be more destruction but the war would go on.' So Japan needed to see Nagasaki obliterated before succumbing to the inevitable. This was the only time in its history that Japan capitulated to a foreign power.

74. Truman Had a 'Do Nothing Congress'

From 1945 to 1953, Truman had to make a number of tough decisions. While the first was the bombing of Japan, others included how much money America should contribute to the rebuilding of Europe, how to handle communist expansion in Europe, China and other areas of Asia, and, finally, whether to declare a new war in Korea. While Truman was certainly busy, his Congress was not.

Throughout that Eightieth Congress, a total of 1,739 bills were passed, compared to the more usual 2,400–2,500. Because of this Truman called it the 'Do Nothing Congress'. This fall in the amount of legislation passed was a sign that the checks and balances created by the Founding Fathers to prevent tyranny were becoming an excuse to block the president of another party from implementing his campaign pledges. However, the 113th Congress in 2013–4 makes the 'Do Nothing Congress' look positively efficient. It passed just 223 bills, showing that Congressional intransigence was only going to get worse. It is a reminder that an American president has less automatic power to get things done than a British Prime Minister, who will usually only come to office as the head of the majority party.

Because Truman was hampered by Congress in fulfilling his goals as president, he spent considerable effort to ensure a majority at the next Congressional election. His investment paid off as the mid-term elections resulted in the Republicans losing a total of seventy-three seats in Congress, enough to make the difference Truman needed.

75. THE KOREAN WAR WAS AMERICA'S FIRST UNSUCCESSFUL FOREIGN WAR

The Korean War (1950–53) is also called the 'forgotten war'. It didn't have anything like the importance of the Second World War and never caught the nation's imagination like Vietnam. John Wayne was the definitive American action hero and film icon of the twentieth century: he 'fought' at the Alamo, in the Second World War, in Vietnam, and even played Genghis Khan, but he couldn't be bothered to make a movie about the Korean War.

The war is important for a number of reasons, but most notably because it is the only time the United Nations has gone to war. While the Americans supplied most of the men and equipment for the war effort (as would become the pattern for all future American military interventions), this was not an 'American' defence of Korea but, instead, a multinational attempt to save the country from a communist takeover by China and the Soviet Union. This three-year war ended in stalemate and resulted in the most heavily defended border and the largest minefield in the world (between North and South Korea).

Truman not only had to make the call to send in troops just five years after the Second World War, he also had to deal with the legendary (and legendarily belligerent) General MacArthur. MacArthur was a heroic figure in the previous conflict, and after overseeing the American occupying administration in Japan, he was regarded as a virtual god in that country. The American population rated him only slightly lower than the Japanese, and it was against this backdrop of popularity and respect that Truman had to go war against his own general.

When the fighting looked bleak for the forces of the UN, MacArthur saved the day by coming up with the high-risk but genius plan of an amphibious assault on

Inchon. It worked and turned the tide of the war in the UN's favour, but as they pushed the North Koreans back to the border with China, Mao unleashed the Chinese army, fresh from its fight for independence. So MacArthur came up with another new and daring plan: he would win the war and push communism out of China ... by nuking China.

MacArthur made the valid point that the Soviets were way behind in their atomic bomb production, so this was the perfect time to strike and go on the offensive with a UN-mandated war. Truman opposed the idea. Not only would the bombing result in millions of deaths, he believed that this would trigger World War III.

MacArthur called in every favour and pulled every trick in the book. He even resorted to having a letter condemning Truman's policy read in the House of Representatives. This was a pivotal yet forgotten moment in American history. Had MacArthur had his way, not only would a new and bigger war have started, he would have undermined the authority of the president. But as America's Commander-in-Chief, President Truman stood his ground and relieved the arrogant MacArthur of his duties. As MacArthur had predicted, the Korean War ended in stalemate.

76. I Like Ike

Truman became increasingly unpopular during his second term, a fact that probably reflected on his vice president, Alben Barkley, who made a bid to become the Democratic nominee in the 1952 election. There was little enthusiasm for Barkley when he got to the Democratic National Convention, where the Democratic Governor of Illinois, Adlai Stevenson (grandson of the earlier vice president), opened the convention with such a good speech that the delegates selected him as their candidate.

Meanwhile, the Republicans sensed that their time had come. Their last president was Herbert Hoover and they had not been in power for twenty years. It was widely expected that MacArthur would run, but instead he endorsed the Ohio senator Robert Taft. This would have ensured Taft's nomination, but another general threw his hat in the ring, Dwight 'Ike' Eisenhower, a popular Second World War hero and NATO commander. In the end, the Republicans had to choose between the isolationist approach to international affairs taken by Taft, or the more liberal internationalist outlook represented by Eisenhower; it was Eisenhower who won the debate.

Eisenhower was over sixty at the time, so to give his campaign some youthful vigour, a forty-year-old senator from California, Richard Nixon, was chosen as his running mate. Eisenhower had led the Allied defeat of Hitler and was seen as a decent and honourable man.

Stevenson, by comparison, was a hard sell. He dithered about running as the Democratic candidate and then appeared aloof to the electorate at large. A gifted orator, he was perceived as being intellectual and progressive, both of which probably worked against him when it came to the voting public.

The election of 1952 harked back twenty years, with the Democrats reminding everyone what Republican President Hoover had done to the economy. It was classic scaremongering, but it was too far back to feel relevant in the booming 1950s. Meanwhile, the Republicans had some scaremongering tactics of their own in the form of Senator Joe McCarthy. This was the era of the witch-hunts for communists because, apparently, they were everywhere.

This was the first campaign to feature television commercials for political parties. The tune 'You Like Ike and I Like Ike' stuck in people's minds and was a catchy piece of political genius (after all, what rhymes with Eisenhower ... power, flower, tower?)

In healthy democracies generally, no matter how well a party is doing, after more than a decade in power the electorate tend to want a change. With Ike's popularity surging, it came as no surprise that the election resulted in an overwhelming victory for the Republicans. Eisenhower won thirty-nine of the forty-eight states and, on 20 January 1953, he was sworn in as America's thirty-fourth president. In a speech dripping with Christian imagery and prayer, he summarised his own beliefs:

> We summon all our knowledge of the past and we scan all signs of the future ... to meet the question: How far have we come in man's long pilgrimage from darkness toward light?

77. Eisenhower Finished off the British Empire ... by Accident

In 1956 Gamal Abdel Nasser, the firebrand leader of Egypt, was making waves about Arab Nationalism, which led to Egypt nationalising the Suez Canal. This was astonishing news to the British and French who had spent a fortune building it and still owned and managed it. However, the Anglo-French partnership had been reaping profits from the canal for the best part of a century, and the canal was ... um ... in Egypt, so why shouldn't it be, y'know, Egyptian? Nasser had a point.

A secret plan was devised by the British, French and Israeli authorities to invade Egypt, depose Nasser and make the Suez Canal a little piece of Britain and France once more. It was classic gunboat diplomacy which, had it happened fifty years earlier, would have been one of those little colonial conflicts everyone (apart from the indigenous population) has subsequently forgotten about. In the event, the invaders tore through the Egyptian forces. The plan had worked perfectly.

However, President Eisenhower was appalled. He had been attempting to calm Nasser and get him to side with the West and America, rather than the Soviet Union, which was also courting this young revolutionary leader. With the Western powers perfectly playing the part of the foreign villain, it was looking like Nasser would willingly go over to Khrushchev and the Soviets.

Meanwhile the Soviets were carrying out an invasion of their own in Hungary, under the pretext of bringing calm to a popular revolution against communist rule. America had no option but to condemn both operations, as anything else would have been seen as political bias and hypocrisy. The bigger problem was that the Soviets were more resistant to threats than Israel and Western Europe. A UN Security Council meeting resulted in serious political and economic pressure on all of the invading nations.

The outcome was the worst of both worlds for western democracy. Firstly, the Soviets successfully crushed the Hungarian Revolution and kept their forces in the country, effectively annexing it. Neither Eisenhower nor the UN could do anything about it; the Iron Curtain had moved further west.

Secondly, just as America had feared, Nasser looked to the Soviet Union to take on the role of protector and defence partner. A potential ally had become a potential enemy.

Thirdly, and most critically, America's political scolding of France and Britain showed them to be much diminished in status. A political scenario like this simply couldn't have happened fifty years earlier, and showed that Britain, in particular, was no longer the world power it had been a generation earlier. Although Britain had lost the subcontinent in 1948, in 1956 it still had an empire and Commonwealth stretching across the globe, but many mark the start of the demise of the British Empire with the Suez Crisis of 1956. British Prime Minister Anthony Eden was forced to resign over the whole sorry mess.

With hindsight, Eisenhower said that his neutering of British power had been the greatest mistake of his presidency.

78. THE 1960 ELECTION WAS WON ON TV

Eisenhower served two terms as president, so come the 1960 election it was time for him to leave the White House. Vice President Richard Nixon was selected as the Republican candidate, the first time in a hundred years an incumbent vice president was chosen (this is surprising because you'd imagine anyone in that role would be a natural choice as successor). Against Nixon was the charismatic John F. Kennedy.

Although the candidates were only four years apart in age, the campaign was seen as the old (Nixon) versus the new (Kennedy). Nixon made the tactical error of visiting all of the now fifty states, including the ones that were always going to vote for him. Kennedy, by comparison, focussed on key battlegrounds and, with his enormous war chest, spent lavishly to secure swing states.

Because he had been vice president for eight years, Nixon chose to talk about his experience; Kennedy emphasized his youth. Nixon grew up poor; Kennedy came from a prominent family and a life of privilege. Nixon had served with honour in the Second World War; Kennedy's patrol boat was sunk and he received an award for heroism by ensuring the survival of his ten-man crew. Nixon was losing the game of one-upmanship against an electrifying speaker who was also one of the best-looking presidential candidates in history.

Perhaps the most memorable moment in the battle between these two very different men was their first televised debate. The majority of those who listened on radio thought that Nixon had won, but an estimated 70 million Americans saw it on TV. Nixon had been struggling with a heavy cold and refused to wear makeup, so he looked sickly and sweaty on screen.

Also, when he was asked a question, he did what was natural and addressed the person who asked it. By contrast, Kennedy looked tanned and relaxed, and when he answered questions he looked into the camera. Nixon had the attention of his questioner; Kennedy had the attention of over 70 million people.

Nixon learned the lessons of this first encounter and upped his game in future debates, but you cannot 'unsee' something, and Nixon's appearance in that first debate led to the light-hearted question, 'Would you buy a used car from this man?' Nixon had lost the image war. The Republicans countered with a whispering campaign that, as a Roman Catholic, Kennedy would have to take orders from the pope. Nevertheless, Kennedy would become America's first Catholic president.

The results in the 1960 election were the closest for generations. Kennedy got 49.72 per cent of the popular vote and Nixon got 49.55 per cent. There were only a little over 100,000 votes in an election where more than 64 million votes were cast. In the end Kennedy won 303 electoral votes to Nixon's 219. Nixon felt Kennedy had stolen the election – understandable after such a close vote – but the truth was that Nixon was outmanoeuvred and hadn't understood that there was a new way to do politics.

79. Kennedy Was Style over Substance

I am aware that I am now writing about presidents who are within living memory and, as such, it's possible to argue that this may not be 'history'. I am also aware that John F. Kennedy is a near-mythical president, but the purpose of the book is to examine facts, so let's examine the record of America's thirty-fifth president.

The Bay of Pigs (April 1961) was a botched attempt to invade Cuba. Led by Cuban dissidents and backed by the CIA, it was little more than the gunboat diplomacy that had been so widely condemned in Egypt less than a decade earlier. It was an ill-conceived plan to which Kennedy agreed.

While the Bay of Pigs was a fiasco, President Kennedy will be remembered for his skilful handling of the 1962 Cuban Missile Crisis when, against the advice of hardliners, he followed his own instincts and averted World War III. At the time, communist Cuba agreed that the Soviets should position nuclear missiles in their country. American security was threatened and the resulting confrontation could well have led to war. After tense negotiations, Khrushchev agreed to remove the missiles in return for US assurances that it would never invade Cuba. Kennedy showed responsible leadership and a determination to find a peaceful solution.

And it was Kennedy who announced that the US would put the first man on the moon, an ambitious objective spoken by a great orator who looked every inch the virile American male. Realisation of this was not to occur in his lifetime, but in announcing the launch of America's space programme, he famously said:

> We choose to go to the moon, not because it is easy, but because it is hard.

It was also Kennedy who watched helplessly as the Berlin Wall was constructed, and while he didn't accelerate American troop deployments to Vietnam, he didn't pull them out either. It seems fair to conclude that his success rate against communism was patchy at best.

Then there were the lies that underpinned an image of the perfect man with the perfect family, everyone living in 'Camelot'. In truth, Kennedy was a voracious womaniser, but JFK and his team were ahead of their time in knowing how to handle the media, disseminate misinformation and keep the myths alive.

Similarly, Kennedy suppressed the fact that he had Addison's disease, suffered from extreme back pain (from earlier back injuries, but not helped by his sexual promiscuity), and took a cocktail of drugs, including amphetamines, to manage it. Like FDR, JFK knew better than to project the image of an unhealthy president and was more than happy to cover things up. While many words can be used to describe Kennedy's presidency, 'Camelot' is not one of them.

The general public knew nothing of the potential scandals, and those who knew kept quiet, but the immortal words of his inauguration address, 'Ask not what your country can do for you; ask what you can do for your country,' inspired a generation.

80. JFK Was Assassinated by Lee Harvey Oswald

While the assassination of President Kennedy in Dallas, Texas on 22 November 1963 did not spark the first conspiracy theory in history, it's the one that has received the most traction, and while it has been superseded by events like the 9/11 conspiracy theory, it was the first one to gain widespread attention. Entire books of *wildly* varying quality have been written on this topic, so I will be brief and dispel a few myths. (If you want an exhaustive look at all this, try Vincent Bugliosi's *Reclaiming History*. Warning: it's longer than *War & Peace*.)

Lee Harvey Oswald might well have chosen a better site for the assassination, but the book depository gave a clear view of JFK's motorcade route and Dealey Plaza, where he shot the president once in the back and once in the head. Contrary to popular belief, Oswald was not a mediocre shot (he was near the top of his class in the marines), and firing three aimed shots from a bolt-action rifle in less than ten seconds is easy if you've had military training. Oswald's plan was less elaborate than that of Charles Guiteau, the man who shot President Garfield.

So what of the magic bullet? Well that's been taken out of context (in books and in the movie *JFK*). John Connally, the Governor of Texas, was sitting in front of Kennedy; he was not *directly* in front of him, but below and to one side, meaning that the trajectory of the bullet that shot Connally would had to have come from behind. The explanation doesn't involve any cover-up or weird physics.

Then there's the grassy knoll: everything about this has been taken out of context from witness statements submitted to the Warren Commission. (Witnesses may have the best of intentions, but there are always inconsistencies. Ask any police officer.) There is no evidence of any group of shadowy men firing from a completely different direction. Also, the acoustic information from a motorcycle policeman's recording turned out to be completely misrepresented; there is no evidence of any echoed gunshots.

And there is no proof to support any theory that anyone other than Oswald was the man pulling the trigger on that day. The more interesting question was *why* did he do it? Was it communist sympathies, or was he a Soviet spy carrying out assassination orders from the Kremlin? Had he been paid by the mafia, or was he simply a crazy guy who thought it was a good idea to kill the president? We'll never know as Oswald was killed by Jack Ruby a few days later. Many assume Ruby was under orders from someone else (more conspiracies), but Americans were overwhelmed by grief at the time, and many would have welcomed a chance to shoot Oswald.

Lincoln was killed by a man who was part of a conspiracy, as was McKinley, but Garfield and Kennedy appear to have been cut down by crazy loners with wild ideas.

81. Lyndon Johnson Was the Eighth Vice President to Fill a Dead Man's Shoes

With the assassination of John Kennedy, an eighth vice president became president on the death of his predecessor. Lyndon B. Johnson, a Texan, had accompanied Kennedy on the trip to Dallas and was sworn in as America's thirty-sixth president just two hours after JFK's death. Johnson was older and came from a far more traditional background than Kennedy. In many ways they were polar opposites, but he had been chosen to help JFK gain support in the South. Johnson proved to be a divisive president, thanks in no small part to his role in the conduct of the Vietnam War, but he also made a big impact on America in positive ways.

Johnson probably would want to be remembered for another war he waged with great vigour, his 'War on Poverty'. Although now largely forgotten, Johnson's presidency was characterised by his moves toward greater social justice, and his legislation lifted millions of Americans out of poverty. In the 1964 election campaign, he promised to create the 'Great Society'. It worked, and he was re-elected with 61 per cent of the popular vote, the widest margin in American electoral history.

What hasn't been forgotten is the counter-intuitive sight of a powerful, white Texan advocating civil rights for African Americans. While President Kennedy had championed racial integration and equal rights for all, it was Johnson who got the ball rolling and passed the effective legislation. The Voting Rights Act of 1965 dismantled many of the southern laws deliberately designed to disenfranchise African Americans. The South was then a segregated society, with separate toilets for whites and blacks, a place where restaurants and buses had 'whites-only' seating. This was very close to Apartheid, the system of segregation based on race that existed in South Africa, which had made that country a pariah in the international community.

Johnson had been in Washington politics for so long that he knew how to get things done, and it was his pragmatic use of political power that got the legislation ratified. He met Martin Luther King, Jr. and other leaders of the civil rights' movement in the White House, showing that his concerns were more than just lip service. All of this culminated in the enormously significant Civil Rights Act of 1968.

Johnson not only had a pragmatic approach to politics, he also had the cunning to get what he wanted. He understood body language and that we all like a bit of space. When someone not invited into your personal space gets too close, it's uncomfortable. Johnson was six feet, four inches tall and, when talking to people would deliberately get very close in order to intimidate them and coerce them into doing what he wanted. This tactic became known as the 'Johnson treatment'. In the Washington political culture of macho competitiveness, there was a rumour that Johnson's ... er ... 'Johnson' was nicknamed 'Jumbo'. He is even on record talking to tailors about giving him more room in that area. True or not, it was another ingenuous tactic.

82. America Fought in the Vietnam War

This is not the place to recount a history of America's involvement in Vietnam, which began with Eisenhower in the 1950s and ended, finally, in 1975. Like much else at the time, the war was sculpted by the images that poured out of televisions, so it felt closer to home than it was.

In the grand scheme of things Vietnam was no more an American defeat than the Korean War in the 1950s or Afghanistan in the twenty-first century. Like those other two wars, America was involving itself in what was a civil war. While it is true that Americans were doing most of the fighting, no new countries were being created. And like almost all wars America has been involved in since the 1960s, America suffered no crushing defeats; but just by continuing to exist, the enemy was seen as winning.

An important difference between now and then: today, most combatants are part of a volunteer standing army. Then, half a million conscripts were sent to fight a vicious war halfway across the globe. These were young men who felt no obligation to keep Vietnam communist free. The resulting controversy meant that Johnson created a veritable civil war in his own country, with families split between backing the war or protesting against it. It was this division that Johnson is remembered for. After dropping more bombs on Vietnam than were dropped in the whole of the Second World War (by all sides), and with over 50,000 dead, America still did not get its way.

83. The 1968 Presidential Election Was Unique

With the rules in place that a sitting president couldn't run for a third term, Johnson stepped down at the end of his second term and the Democrats chose Johnson's vice president, Hubert Humphrey, as their candidate. The Republicans brought back Richard Nixon, who beat the Governor of California, an ex-actor called Ronald Reagan, for the nomination. What made this election unusual was the strong showing of a third party. Thanks to television, the American Independent Party and its candidate, George Wallace, were able to advocate the return of segregation to the South.

The 1968 election was played out against another backdrop of tragedies: The Vietnam War still raged and both the Civil Rights leader Martin Luther King, Jr. and the Democratic hopeful, Robert Kennedy (JFK's brother), had been assassinated. There had been extensive anti-war protests, riots in the streets, and, symbolised by the 1967 'Summer of Love', the counterculture was on the rise.

Nixon, who eight years earlier had so narrowly lost to John Kennedy, promised to restore calm to the nation and find a new way of dealing with the increasingly unpopular war in Vietnam. In the summer Humphrey was behind Nixon by over 10 per cent, but he increased his popularity by appealing to the unions and attacking the barely concealed racist ideologies of George Wallace.

Wallace won nearly 10 million votes, but it was a close race between the Republicans (43.4 per cent) and the Democrats (42.7 per cent). By a small margin, Richard Nixon became the thirty-seventh president.

84. RICHARD NIXON WAS A CROOK

Richard Nixon will always be remembered for his role in the 'Watergate Affair', the illegal break-in and subsequent bugging of the Democratic Party headquarters in the Watergate Hotel in Washington D.C. When the scandal first broke, Nixon denied any role and declared, 'I'm not a crook!' The fact that it was illegal and that Nixon knew about it (even if he did not sanction it) led to his eventual resignation before he was almost certainly impeached.

It's history's job to look at events dispassionately, and while the scandal points to a flaw in Nixon's character, this was not the only thing he did in his presidency. It should not be forgotten that when Neil Armstrong spoke to the president from the moon, it was Nixon on the other end of the line. Nixon didn't start the space race or initiate the Apollo Missions, but he continued to fund them (a speech had been prepared in the event of the mission's failure and the deaths of the astronauts, showing it was a high-risk mission, which Nixon cleared to go ahead). However, due to cost, he did veto a permanent moon base.

The Vietnam War also reflects the good and the bad in Nixon's presidency. He ordered the secret bombing of Cambodia and other clandestine operations in Laos. He didn't do these things because he wanted to break international law but because the North Vietnamese army had covertly leaked into these countries. It was a pragmatic if ignoble solution to the fighting. This was not the only time he carried out such secret interventions: in the late 60s and early 70s, South America was awash with covert CIA operations against communist groups.

However, on the more positive side, he was the president who oversaw the end of combat operations in Vietnam. The Paris Peace Accords (signed in 1973) ended direct US military intervention and called for a ceasefire between North and South Vietnam. Nixon was better at diplomacy than bombing. This was evident when he opened up a dialogue with Chairman Mao and communist China. Nixon recognised that, despite having fundamentally different political ideologies, it was better to have a conversation with the most populous nation on Earth than to pretend they didn't exist. This was a nuanced and successful diplomatic plan.

On the domestic front, the economy was not doing well when Nixon took over the reins in 1969, but he fought hard to bring inflation down. He wanted to implement 'New Federalism', an attempt to centralise some of the decision-making, but Congress put the brakes on that. His economic policies were ultimately scuppered by the 1973 Oil Crisis, when the whole developed world was, in essence, held to ransom by the Arab oil producers. The result was shortages and a huge spike in oil prices. There was not a lot Nixon could do about this, but it happened on his watch.

Nixon left the White House on 9 August 1974, despised by virtually everyone. He went into forced retirement, a bitter man.

85. GERALD FORD WAS THE BEST LOOKING PRESIDENT

The above title is a bold statement, but it can be backed up. In his youth Gerald Ford was an (American) football player and quite the all-round athlete. He caught the eye of a photographer and went on to do some catalogue modelling before taking the path to a more serious career.

Spiro Agnew (the best name *ever* for an American vice president) had been Nixon's first vice president, but he had been forced to resign in 1973 after being engulfed in a sea of corruption allegations. In an unprecedented situation, Gerald Ford, who was the House Minority Leader at the time, became the new vice president under the terms of the Twenty-fifth Amendment. As a vice president but also as a president, Ford was always Plan B (he is the only man to have become both without being voted into either office). When Nixon resigned in 1974, the ex-model became the America's thirty-eighth president and the most powerful man on the planet.

Ford was aware of the incongruence of his position – that he was the head of a democracy without having been elected by the nation. In his first address to the nation he said:

> I am acutely aware that you have not elected me as your president ... so I ask you to confirm me as your president with your prayers.

But not even the Almighty could save this presidency. Ford was just a bland non-event in a presidency rocked by the fallout of the Watergate scandal, a country nursing its wounded pride after an ineffective intervention in Vietnam, and an economy suffering the worst recession since the Great Depression of the 1930s.

Ford chose Nelson Rockefeller as his vice president over a young George Bush (Sr), but he was loyal to his old boss, giving Richard Nixon a full and unconditional pardon to avoid the potentially disastrous fallout of an impeachment. The move aroused much suspicion and condemnation and was deeply unpopular at the time. In such a short presidency, the hostility Gerald Ford inspired can be best illustrated by the fact that there were two assassination attempts within seventeen days of each other ... and, unusually, both shooters were women.

With such an atmosphere of animosity, it was surprising that the Republicans wanted him to run in the 1976 presidential election. To be fair to Ford, even he doubted his chances of getting a second term. He beat his main rival, Ronald Reagan, in the primaries, but his heart wasn't in the campaign, and with an election in November he didn't hit the campaign trail until October. As it was, the election results were much closer than the above information would suggest; however, as close as it was, Ford lost to Jimmy Carter, which allowed the Democrats to return to the White House.

Gerald Ford is a minor president in the pantheon of American leaders, but he has the distinction of being the president who lived the longest. He died in 2006 at the age of ninety-three.

86. JIMMY CARTER WAS A DEMOCRAT FROM THE DEEP SOUTH

Many presidents are lawyers, a few are military men, but only one was a peanut farmer. James Earl Carter, always known as 'Jimmy', was the peanut farmer who got into politics and rose through the ranks of the Georgia legislature to become the state's governor by 1971. His first Executive Order as America's thirty-ninth president was an unconditional pardon for the draft evaders who went 'missing' during the Vietnam War; it was his way of drawing a line under the years of division. In the same year he signed the bill that bailed out the car manufacturer Chrysler. The use of government money to prop up a private company was neither the 'American way', nor was it sound free market economics, but it was necessary as the country continued to lurch from one fuel crisis to another recession. The logic was simple: Chrysler employed thousands, and it was better to keep these people in work than to allow a key company to go bankrupt and leave thousands without jobs.

During Carter's presidency, America's economy grew by an overall average of 3.4 per cent, which was about normal for a developed country at that time. However, his presidency can be viewed as a game of two halves: the first half showed a strong recovery from the recession that had occurred under Ford, but the second half saw yet another energy crisis (caused this time by the Iranian Revolution in 1979) and double-digit inflation. In other words, all of the hard work of the first half was undone by external and largely unforeseeable factors in the second half. Because of this, Carter ordered painful budget cuts, with America's military losing $6 billion, a move that did not sit well with many in Washington and beyond.

The Second World War marked the last time in its history that America was not dependent on oil imports, but it was the early 1970s that revealed how vulnerable the nation was to fluctuations in its price. The search was on for alternatives. Nuclear power was looking like a good option until March 1979, when the Three Mile Island nuclear reactor suffered a meltdown, which turned out to be the worst accident in US nuclear power history. The result of this was that fossil fuels were now regarded as the only option, and, therefore, the flow of oil was to continue.

Although Carter can be seen as a hostage to external factors beyond his control, it was entirely his choice that the United States should boycott the Moscow Olympic Games in 1980. The move was made following the Soviet Union's invasion of Afghanistan in 1979, but it was an extremely controversial decision which bitterly disappointed many athletes. Sixty-four other nations joined the boycott, making it a much diminished Olympic games, something the Soviets were to remember come the Los Angeles Olympics in 1984.

Jimmy Carter, like all Presidents, meant well, but a mixture of bad luck and some less-than-popular decisions led to his defeat in the 1980 presidential election.

87. OPERATION EAGLE CLAW MADE CARTER LOOK LIKE A LOSER

The British use mundane names to disguise military plans. For example, Operation Market Garden was the name for the mass aerial drop of troops into the Netherlands in 1944. The Nazis also used bland names: Case Blue was the attempted invasion of the Caucasus. The idea was that even if you knew the name of the plan, you couldn't guess what it was about. The Americans, however, always like a little razzmatazz. Operation Rolling Thunder was the mass bombing of Vietnam, and in 1980 President Jimmy Carter approved Operation Eagle Claw.

In 1979 Iran was convulsed in revolution by Islamic hardliners, led by the charismatic Ayatollah Khomeini. The hated shah was deposed, which was a problem for the West as he had been an ally, and the new regime hated everything Western. This led to an unacceptable breach of international law when protestors (covertly supported by the new regime) stormed the American Embassy in Tehran and took fifty-two embassy staff hostage.

No country could tolerate such an outrage. This was the height of the Cold War, and yet American diplomatic staff were posted in Moscow, and similarly, Soviet diplomats could go about their business in Washington D.C. It was simply unheard of for any country to take hostage another nation's diplomatic staff; it was anathema. So the Americans devised a plan to secretly deploy their special forces: they would fly in and storm the embassy compound where the hostages were being held, free them from their captors (called 'extraction' by the military), put them on helicopters and fly them out to aircraft waiting in the secret Desert One base in the middle of the Iranian desert.

The big problem was the remoteness of the Desert One base and the erratic weather of the desert. On the day of the operation there were so many mechanical failures affecting both the airplanes and helicopters that President Carter ordered the mission to be aborted before it had gone into the extraction phase.

Before abandoning their mission and evacuating the area, the American forces destroyed the useless aircraft, leaving the Iranians with a giant PR coup when images of burnt-out US military equipment were broadcast around the world. The American projection of power was dented once again. First it was Vietnam, then, just over a decade later, a botched rescue attempt in Iran. America needed a PR coup of its own.

It was in the same year and against this background that the nation entered a presidential election. Ronald Reagan, the Republican candidate, intended to make America great again (a message that Donald Trump would use decades later) and ran on a message of hope. Reagan won by a landslide, taking forty-four of the fifty states.

After holding them for fourteen months, Iran finally released the fifty-two American hostages on the last day of Carter's presidency.

Carter fared better as an ex-president. He was awarded the 2002 Nobel Peace Prize 'for his decades of untiring effort to find peaceful solutions to international conflicts'.

88. Ronald Reagan Was Effective in Foreign Affairs

As the American economy recovered in the 1980s, so too did America's international standing and reputation. Like President Reagan, British Prime Minister Margaret Thatcher was also on the political right, and the two got on famously, their foreign policies largely fitting hand-in-glove.

Reagan was America's fortieth president and the first since the Vietnam War to carry out extensive overseas military campaigns. When the legitimate government of Grenada (a small Caribbean island nation) was overthrown in a communist coup, the president sent in US troops. The communists never stood a chance, and because there was no way for this conflict to escalate to the levels of Vietnam, it was always going to be a one-sided victory. This was a boost for American military prestige.

Reagan wasn't so lucky in Lebanon. The Middle East, always a pressure cooker of religious and sectarian tensions, occasionally boils over, with bloody results. Reagan deployed the marines in an attempt to calm Lebanon's brutal war. However, when a suicide bomber drove an explosives-laden truck into the US compound, it killed 241 and wounded another 60. While the US Navy shelled the coast, the Americans pulled out by way of Syria.

Perhaps Reagan's biggest failure was his 'War on Drugs'. When crack cocaine hit the streets of America, billions of dollars were poured into South American governments in an attempt to stem the flow. Having already cost countless lives, the unofficial war continues to this day – and the drug trade is still booming.

However, Reagan's single greatest triumph was his handling of the Soviet Union. His tactics involved a clever mix of grandstanding, a little bit of sabre rattling and plenty of dialogue around peace. One of the best examples of his provocative but hopeful speeches came in Germany as the president stood in front of the Brandenburg Gate. The gate, walled off on the communist side of the Berlin Wall, had become a symbol of the division, not just of Berlin but of Germany as a whole. The imagery was powerful and Reagan addressed not just the audience in front of him, but the Soviet leader, Mikhail Gorbachev, as well:

> General Secretary Gorbachev, if you seek peace, if you seek prosperity for the Soviet Union and Eastern Europe, if you seek liberalisation, come here to this gate. Mr. Gorbachev, open this gate. Mr. Gorbachev, tear down this wall.

While the fall of the Berlin Wall and the collapse of the Soviet Union happened after Reagan's presidency, by the 1980s America looked re-energised compared to the crumbling façade of the Soviet bloc. This was in no small way due to the energy and passion of the oldest president in history.

From 1985 to 1988 Reagan held four summits with Gorbachev. These resulted in partial nuclear disarmament by the two superpowers. Led by the most charismatic president since John Kennedy, America not only felt strong, it was strong once again. Was it any surprise that, in 1984, Ronald Reagan was re-elected by all but one of the fifty states?

89. RONALD REAGAN SYMBOLISED THE 1980s

Franklin Roosevelt and Ronald Reagan aren't often compared, but there are similarities in their first terms of office: they both inherited a demoralised nation, and there was a feeling that the country had lost its way. In both cases the presidents' solutions had less to do with policy and more to do with image. Some presidents are respected, others are despised, but both Reagan and FDR were the rare presidents who were loved by the masses.

Reagan (again, just like FDR) knew how to project a desirable image. This was unsurprising as his early career had been in radio and, later, as an actor in Hollywood movies. This is where the paths of the two presidents diverge. Ronald Reagan was not a towering intellectual, nor did he claim to be. Instead, Ronald Reagan symbolised a new image for America's president. In the late twentieth and early twenty-first centuries, the British are said to have elected prime ministers who represented people's aspirations – a role model, a person they admired. Americans, by contrast, were now leaning towards someone they felt comfortable with, someone they could have a beer with. Indeed, in recent times some presidential hopefuls have been slammed for being elitist or too intellectual, as if being smart and well-educated were bad things in the leader of the world's most powerful nation.

However, to disparage Reagan just because he never went to university and once starred in a movie with a chimpanzee is doing a disservice to the man. He had hung up his acting credentials long before he became president, having been Governor of California for eight years (from 1967). In the world of the 1980s, just looking and saying the right things on TV could make greater impact on the general population than any piece of legislation.

At sixty-nine, Ronald Reagan is the oldest person to have ever been elected president. His age was raised in the later 1984 presidential election, when the Democrat Walter Mondale said that Reagan was too old to be re-elected. During a television debate, Reagan came back with a brilliantly neutralising line: 'I will not make age an issue of this campaign. I am not going to exploit, for political purposes, my opponent's youth and inexperience.'

Even Mondale thought it was a good line and refrained from mentioning it again.

Reagan continued to use the media in an effective way. His retreats to his ranch and photos of him dressed as a cowboy made him appear to be the very embodiment of America. Another representation of the nation's psyche at the time was the action films coming out of Hollywood. Perhaps the most jingoistic of all was *Rambo: First Blood Part II*. In the film Sylvester Stallone's muscular Vietnam veteran almost singlehandedly re-fights the Vietnam War ... and wins! When Reagan was asked (in 1985) about any future hostage situations he replied with, 'Boy, after seeing "Rambo" last night, I know what to do the next time this happens.'

One line blurred Hollywood with real-world political policy.

90. Reagan Forgot to Duck

This book has been littered with accounts of the assassination attempts of American presidents, and while nefarious groups and individuals continue to plot, the most recent American president to be hit by an assassin's bullet was Ronald Reagan.

John Hinckley, Jr. was a man obsessed with both Jodie Foster and the movie *Taxi Driver* in which the lead character (played by Robert De Niro) plots to assassinate a politician. Hinckley originally planned to hijack a plane and later thought of assassinating Jimmy Carter, but it happened to be the newly elected Ronald Reagan who got in his crosshairs.

On 30 March 1981, at the Hilton Hotel in Washington D.C., Hinckley pulled out a .22 revolver and managed to fire six times at the president. Hinckley wounded both police officer Thomas Delahanty and Secret Service agent Timothy McCarthy, and critically wounded Press Secretary James Brady. Technically, Hinckley missed Reagan, but as the Secret Service agents pushed Reagan into the waiting limo, they inadvertently pushed him into the path of a ricochet that had bounced off the car and penetrated the president's chest.

Reagan was in critical condition when he arrived at the hospital but quipped to his wife, Nancy, 'Honey, I forgot to duck.' Reagan would go on to make a full recovery. Hinckley was arrested, tried and found 'not guilty by reason of insanity'. He remains under institutional psychiatric care.

In the last months of his administration, there were rumours that Reagan was suffering from dementia, but this was never officially confirmed.

91. Bush Senior Won Two Wars

In 1988, Ronald Reagan stepped down and the Republicans chose his vice president, George H. W. Bush, as their candidate. The Democrats selected Michael Dukakis, who managed to run a shambolic race against Bush and was roundly beaten on Election Day. It seems logical for vice presidents to become their party's next presidential candidate, but Bush was the first sitting vice president to be elected president since Martin Van Buren in 1836.

The forty-first President of the United States was not instrumental in the fall of the Soviet Union and the Eastern Bloc, but he was the president when it happened. The collapse of communism in Europe is a book in its own right, so allow me the briefest summary: communism, in its purest form, doesn't work in a complex industrialised economy. Long-term, all the West had to do was wait until this ambitious project floundered as inefficient state-run businesses and organisations crumbled. When the end came, Bush was in position to claim a victory for both democracy and the free market economy.

However, Russia still had enough military equipment to start a war, so President Bush and Chairman Gorbachev declared a US–Russian strategic partnership, which officially marked the end of the Cold War and led to the Strategic Arms Reduction Treaty (START I), another reduction in the world's nuclear arsenal. The Cold War, which had lasted some forty years, was over, and George Bush was the American president who could claim this monumental victory.

Meanwhile, the Middle East exploded into political crisis once again, but this particular crisis was unusual. Saddam Hussein, the dictator of Iraq (and once an American ally), invaded is neighbour Kuwait, a country up until then almost nobody had heard of. Kuwait was small but possessed vast reserves of oil and natural gas. These reserves, combined with the oil from Iraq, suddenly made Saddam the man with a gun to the head of the oil industry.

For those who believe that the subsequent Gulf War was 'all about oil', they are right; but when it's the world's most valuable commodity, vital to all developed economies, it would be naive to think that countries like America wouldn't defend their interests. It's also worth pointing out that Saddam had invaded a sovereign nation, and the UN passed multiple resolutions which not only condemned the invasion but called for a multi-national invasion of Kuwait to eject Saddam's forces. The Gulf War was a coalition of nations fighting on America's side, and was the largest war America had fought since Vietnam. No one knows why Saddam tried to fight a conventional war against a force that was larger and better equipped. Promising the 'mother of all battles', Iraq suffered the 'mother of all defeats'.

The Gulf War succeeded in wiping away the painful memories of Vietnam, secured the oil fields of the Middle East and garnered major support across the free (and some of the less free) world. How could George Bush possibly lose the 1992 election?

92. George H. W. Bush Failed to Win a Second Term

After the heady heights achieved during President Bush's first administration, it would be safe to assume that he was the obvious candidate to win the 1992 presidential election. Immediately after the Gulf War in 1991, Bush's approval ratings were an astonishing 90 per cent. However, just a year later they had slumped to 64 per cent. America was in recession, and the general electorate, with the attention span of goldfish, was never that impressed with foreign policy successes. The fall of the Soviet Union seemed so ... well ... so 1980s. This was 1992 and there was a new kid in town.

William Jefferson Blythe III, known to history as Bill Clinton (after his father died, he took his stepfather's surname), was the young, handsome and dynamic Democratic nominee. His campaign strategist, James Carville, summarised Clinton's campaign strategy in just one sentence: 'It's the economy, stupid.'

James and Bill recognised that securing America's oil supply or ending the Cold War were topics already consigned to history; they wouldn't win the election. Going back to Fact 69, voters care about how things affect them personally, and in 1992 money was tight and President Bush was to blame. While Clinton kept hammering him about the economy, Bush himself was haunted by a memorable phrase he had used at the 1988 Republican Convention: 'Read my lips, no new taxes.'

This had been music to the ears of the party faithful ... except that with expensive foreign wars and a country in recession, there was a justifiable need for tax increases. However, this blatant U-turn angered those who had voted Republican; they had no reason to trust President Bush any more.

A man called Ross Perot ran as an independent in 1992, but as is the usual case for a third-party candidate in America, his campaign was a failure, and he won no states in the election.

During the campaign, Clinton was accused of infidelity (more on that later) as well as having dodged the Vietnam draft (an accusation that was also thrown at Bush's vice president, Dan Quayle). When Clinton was accused of smoking cannabis, his response was, 'I didn't inhale.' This was not to be the only time Clinton was careful with his words, but, if anything, this apparent vulnerability made him more appealing to the average American, rather than less.

Meanwhile, Bush conducted a very old-fashioned campaign. By contrast to Clinton's draft dodging, he was to be the last president to have served in the Second World War, an interesting fact but something that felt irrelevant in the 1990s.

Clinton went on to win by a landslide, taking thirty-two states to Bush's eighteen. All of George Bush's historic work had ultimately counted for nothing, and in a way, his presidency marked the end of the 'old' Republican Party. While the seeds had already been sown by 1992, the fundamentalist Christians, who had previously turned their back on politics, were now becoming more involved in Republican politics, and it was Bill Clinton who stoked their anger.

93. Bill Clinton Scored Many Victories

Bill Clinton became Governor of Arkansas at the age of just thirty-three and, apart from two years, he held the position from 1979 to 1992. Another lawyer who became president, he studied at both Yale (where he met Hillary Rodham, whom he later married) and Oxford University. Clinton was considered to be smart, charismatic and a great orator. America's forty-second president was elected in 1992, and, at the age of forty-six, he was the youngest president since Kennedy.

One of President Clinton's greatest achievements was to drag the US government into a budget surplus in 1998. He managed to get rid of the budget deficit through cost savings and increased taxes on the rich while also reducing the taxes paid by the lowest income families. This was no small achievement. For decades, both before and after Clinton, other presidents have been unable to achieve anything like this as they are either unable or unwilling to make the necessary changes to federal finances.

Clinton may have been tough about balancing the books, but he really wanted the country to grow through trade. He led the way on the North American Free Trade Agreement (NAFTA), a trilateral alliance designed to ease trade among the nations of Canada, Mexico and the United States.

There were forty-six mass shootings at schools in America in the 1990s, with a total of eighty-two dead. The United States has always had an unusually close relationship with firearms thanks to the slightly ambiguous phrasing of the Second Amendment, which gives Americans the 'right to bear arms'. The National Rifle Association makes sure that it's very hard to pass more stringent gun laws, but Clinton was able to pass the Brady Bill, which imposed a five-day waiting period on handgun purchases. It was a small victory, but every little bit is a move in the right direction.

Militarily, there were interventions in the Balkans and Somalia, but they were minor compared to those of both his predecessor and his successor. Instead, Clinton followed in Nixon's footsteps internationally in further normalising America's relationship with China. In the Middle East he came close to bringing together the two, usually intractable, sides of the Israel–Palestine conflict. A deal seemed to be within reach during the 2000 Camp David Summit, and, although there was no final agreement, it was a sign of Clinton's charisma and diplomatic prowess that such constructive talks have not been matched since.

President Clinton's wife took on an unusually politically active role for a First Lady. At the tail end of her husband's presidency, Hillary became a senator from New York, and a political dynasty was born.

Bill Clinton should be remembered as the man who balanced the books, grew the economy and built bridges across the globe. Smart, funny and, arguably, the first 'cool' President, he's up there with the greatest Democratic Presidents. However Bill Clinton is human, and every human has weaknesses, so it is for his greatest weakness, rather than his successes, that he is remembered.

94. Clinton Did Not Have Sexual Relations with That Woman

Bill Clinton and Richard Nixon rarely get compared, but to this author they are echoes of each other. Both were, at the very least, 'good' presidents; they each had a record of notable achievements in their presidencies, and yet, each man's legacy is overshadowed by a specific scandal.

There are some who say that Nixon's involvement in the illegal bugging of opponents' party headquarters is worse than Bill Clinton having an affair with a young woman, but they are missing a very important legal issue. Perjury is a crime, a serious crime. Bill Clinton, then forty-nine, when pressed on whether or not he had had an affair with the twenty-two-year-old Monica Lewinski, famously stated:

I did not have sexual relations with that woman.

This book is not the place to examine the details of what was a sordid mess, but as the evidence mounted it became clear that the president had, indeed, had a sexual fling with Lewinski. By testifying otherwise *under oath*, he had committed perjury. As a lawyer, he tried arguing semantics about whether the term 'sexual relations' applied to what he and Lewinski did. Before you even begin to examine issues of morality, age difference or the abuse of power, Clinton was a perjurer.

Like Nixon, Clinton faced impeachment proceedings, which overshadowed the latter years of his second term. And, again like Nixon, he dodged what seemed to be the inevitable, in Clinton's case by being acquitted. It was an inglorious end to an otherwise successful presidency.

95. It Felt like George W. Bush Was the Worst President of All Time: Part 1

George W. Bush (or 'Dubya' as he is known by his critics) was America's forty-third president. He was not the smartest president, nor did he have the most distinguished career in law or the military. Instead this 'born-again' Governor of Texas had the considerable advantage of being the son and namesake of the most recent Republican president. This Bush was not the first well-connected man to make it to the White House, nor did his policies drive the country into the ground like so many of the ineffectual presidents in the second half of the nineteenth century, but his unsophisticated world view and his abysmal public speaking divided the country in a way not seen since the Vietnam War years.

The mistakes Bush made in some of his speeches are breathtaking and were further exacerbated in an era of smartphones and social media. Here are just two examples:

> Our enemies are innovative and resourceful, and so are we. They never stop thinking about new ways to harm our country and our people, and neither do we.
>
> A lot of times in politics you have people look you in the eye and tell you what's not on their mind.

These are easy to mock, but poor public speaking is no more a sign of low intelligence than exceptional rhetoric is a sign of moral rectitude.

On 11 September 2001, just a few months into his presidency, Bush was reading to school children when he was quietly told that the nation was under attack. The filmed footage shows him trying to work out what to do next. To immediately leave would seem to be the obvious thing to do, but he sits there, visibly struggling with some kind of internal monologue. If there was one moment that determined Bush would never be seen as a great president, this was it. But this doesn't mean he was the worst president, either.

Everyone remembers what it was like on September 11, 2001: terrifying and confusing, with misinformation making everything worse. However, the images of the World Trade Centre's collapsing twin towers mean Bush will always be the president on whose watch the most devastating terrorist attack in human history took place.

Bush's first response was to send troops into Afghanistan, where the terrorist leader Osama bin Laden was known to be hiding. This made complete sense. An attack on the scale of 9/11 required more than just the deployment of cruise missiles. Americans were in a state of shock similar to that after the attack on Pearl Harbor, which had resulted in a similar number of casualties. Troops *had* to be deployed, and the subsequent fighting was tough in a region where, just over a decade earlier, the Soviet Union had been defeated.

If it can be argued that the war in Afghanistan made sense, the later invasion of Iraq was a disaster for everyone concerned. The fallout from this ill-conceived debacle will go on for decades.

96. It Felt like George W. Bush Was the Worst President of All Time: Part 2

George W. Bush's presidency got off to a rocky start when the vote results in the 2000 election were so close that it took a Supreme Court decision to resolve the matter. The key state of Florida was the battleground where the less-than-convincing results were challenged by Bush's Democratic rival, Al Gore. Although Bush lost the popular vote, the Supreme Court ruled that he had won the election (electoral votes again). Convinced that Providence was on their side, right-wing Republican Christians breathed a sigh of relief while disgruntled Democrats believed the result had less to do with Providence and more to do with dubious voting practices in Florida.

Bush was settling into his presidency when 9/11 happened. The events of that day resulted in two foreign wars. However, as ill-conceived as at least one of these wars were, the most damning charge against Bush concerned his failure in domestic policy. In the last months of his presidency, Bush was at the helm during the single biggest economic collapse since the stock market crash of 1929. But unlike 9/11, the signs had been there. When the credit crunch hit the financial markets in 2008, the US lost 2.6 million jobs.

Just as the whole edifice of communism teetered on the brink of collapse in the early 1990s, so too did the free market economies in 2008–2009, when the markets were swimming in a sea of toxic assets and sub-prime mortgages. A pivotal moment came when Lehman Brothers, a global financial firm, filed for bankruptcy with bank debts of $613 billion and bond debts of $155 billion (roughly as much debt as the annual GDP of Switzerland); the term 'too big to fail' was born. Taking their lead from British Prime Minister Gordon Brown, Bush and the US Treasury quickly came up with government relief needed to shore up the banks and rebuild confidence in the markets. It stopped a catastrophe from turning into a meltdown.

It has been forgotten that this Bush championed $1.3 trillion of tax cuts, significantly lowering the marginal tax rates for nearly all US taxpayers. He passed Medicare Part D, which expanded federally funded health care benefits. He also launched a $15 billion AIDS program to combat the disease in the US and Africa. He was a more socially aware president than he is given credit for.

Hurricane Katrina was nobody's fault, but the near Biblical destruction of New Orleans meant colossal rescue and repair plans were urgently needed. Bush charged the Federal Emergency Management Agency (FEMA) with responsibility for the aftermath, but FEMA's response was slow, making it seem as if Bush didn't care. This wasn't true, but in the age of TV, Facebook and YouTube, the appearance of presidential callousness was everywhere.

Recessions, wars, natural disasters – none of these things were unique to Bush's presidency, but his took place during the multimedia age, when everything is examined under a microscope. How many other presidents would have survived such scrutiny?

97. 2008 WAS AN HISTORIC ELECTION

Before the presidential primaries of 2008, all the smart money was on Hillary Clinton. The former First Lady had been busily positioning herself in the corridors of power for most of a decade, and she fully intended to become the Democratic nominee in 2008. However, the smart money was not so smart on this occasion.

Seemingly from out of nowhere, a young black senator from Illinois began electrifying the crowds. His name should have been toxic: in American political circles, Barack Hussein Obama was the most foreign-sounding name since Martin Van Buren. Worse still, his middle name was the same as Saddam Hussein's surname, while to others 'Obama' reminded them of Osama, the Al-Qaeda leader responsible for 9/11. It would be like trying to get elected in 1945 Britain with the name Hitler Napoleon von Kaiserton. And yet people saw past the superficial differences and were mesmerised by the greatest orator of his generation, and the man who would become the Democratic candidate.

By contrast, the Republicans were rolling out the usual suspects and eventually settled on the long-serving Senator from Arizona, John McCain. McCain, a naval pilot in Vietnam, had been captured and tortured by the North Vietnamese. In any other election he would have been a strong contender for the White House. It was his bad luck to run against the charismatic version of a nuclear weapon; McCain looked hopelessly out-of-date and old-fashioned. To boost the Republican image, he cast around for a running mate and chose the fiery and media friendly Sarah Palin, whose ear for a controversial soundbite gave hope to the Christian right; she looked like the perfect riposte to Obama. The resulting ticket meant that no matter who won, a first would happen in November 2008: either America would have its first black president or it would have its first female vice president.

Obama campaigned on a promise of change, on being someone uncorrupted by decades spent on Capitol Hill, an outsider working for the disenfranchised. Multicoloured posters of his face were everywhere underscored with just one word: 'Hope'. Palin, by comparison, saw her star fade almost as quickly as it had arrived. Like Obama, she was also a Washington outsider; however, unlike Obama, she didn't know much about ... well ... anything. An example was her claim she could see Russia from her house in Alaska. She couldn't.

As the presidential race peaked so did the financial crisis, and McCain put his campaign on hold to return to Washington to help solve it. It quickly became obvious that he wasn't going to solve anything and had succeeded only in losing momentum against a rival who was filling stadia with his inspirational speeches.

It was clear what the electorate wanted, and the result was a decisive win for Barack Obama. This was remarkable considering that less than 150 years since the abolition of slavery, when segregation was still within living memory, a person of colour was now the forty-fourth President of the United States.

98. Be Careful What You Wish for ...

Barack Obama (yet another lawyer) was elected on a tidal wave of optimism. However as Obama talked about hope, Sarah Palin and her newly formed Tea Party (in reference to the Boston colonial riots against British taxation) talked about outrage and fear. For the time being, the Tea Party would be seen merely as a group of political eccentrics. Meanwhile, Obama had a country to run, and he was determined to reach out across the political divide to secure bipartisan approval for a number of his innovative ideas. This was to be his downfall.

While both the political left and right in America wanted an outsider to shake up what was seen by everyone as a corrupt Washington, controlled more by special interest groups than voter concerns, the problem is that there are not a lot of ways into a group if you are a self-proclaimed outsider. President Lyndon Johnson (Fact 81) was able to pass unpopular legislation because he was a decades-long insider. He knew how Washington worked and was able to call in favours.

President Obama had only limited experience of Washington politics, and as many of his ideas were clearly anathema to the Republican right wing, the party did everything in its power to block proposed legislation. As Fact 74 mentioned, Truman was frustrated with his 'do nothing' Congress, and yet the recent 114th Congress passed even fewer laws. The Founding Fathers' noble system of checks and balances was used as the means to a congressional standoff.

The problem was exemplified by healthcare reform. In his campaign, Obama had promised substantial improvements in healthcare provisions to include, among other things, those who had had no previous medical coverage. So after dealing with the financial crisis, healthcare reform was the new president's first priority. But the legislation he proposed created difficulties within his own party (congressional representatives were getting complaints of 'socialism' from their constituents) and downright opposition from the Republicans. His blandly named Patient Protection and Affordable Care Act of 2010 was dubbed 'Obamacare' and was passed only after lengthy debates in both houses of Congress (and a great deal of horse trading). That the bill was passed at all was due only to the fact that in the first two years of his presidency Obama had a majority in Congress. If things were bad then, they would only get worse when the Republicans won a majority in the next congressional election.

Every piece of proposed Democratic legislation met opposition from the Republican Party in general and from its increasingly influential Tea Party offshoot in particular. This included their refusal to approve the budget legislation necessary for the government to continue to function. In one instance, the federal government shut down for sixteen days before the bill was passed.

Despite all the antics in Washington and the portrayal of the president by right-wing news channels as only slightly less dangerous than a terrorist, Barack Obama was re-elected in 2012.

99. President Obama Is the Best President at Playing Hide and Seek

While domestic policy was mired in indecision and Republican fury, President Obama, like most presidents, found it easier to get his way with foreign policy. His presidency witnessed an increasingly complex international picture, only gradual global economic recovery, the continuing rise of China, the Arab Spring and its aftermath, and the growth of terrorist organisations like ISIS. None of these problems are unprecedented but none of them have simple solutions.

Right off the bat, Obama inherited two wars, which he ended for America by withdrawing all US combat troops from Iraq and Afghanistan (America's longest war at over thirteen years). After the Bush, Jr. Presidency portrayed America as an international bully, Obama did much to restore the nation's prestige in the eyes of key allies. Obama had promised in his election campaign to dismantle Camp X-Ray in Guantanamo Bay, but without the cooperation of Congress he found the way obstructed (and at the time of writing 'Gitmo' is still an issue).

America's response to the unprecedented popular uprising stretching across North Africa and into the Middle East was muted. After fighting two wars in Islamic countries with questionable results, it was reluctant to become involved again (and didn't want to be seen as being part of a so-called 'clash of civilisations'). Although the American contribution to air strikes in places like Libya and Syria has been sizeable, more reliance was placed on its allies, most notably France and Britain.

However, it is 2 May 2011 that marks this president's greatest military success. After a decade of searching, American intelligence agencies thought they had found

Osama bin Laden, the Al-Qaeda leader who was responsible for the 9/11 attacks.

Bin Laden was hiding in a compound in Abbottabad near a Pakistani military academy. Seal Team 6 was deployed and carried out a raid which resulted in bin Laden's death and the confiscation of significant amounts of intelligence. The operation wasn't a complete success as one of the helicopters crashed, so not everything they found could be taken away. While most of the classified equipment was successfully destroyed, the whole world caught a glimpse of America's new infiltration (stealth) helicopter. It was the PR coup of the decade. Bin Laden's body was taken back to a base to be formally identified and later given an Islamic burial at sea. Pretty much everyone except Al-Qaeda and Amnesty International were happy with the outcome.

Obama spoke to the nation after the operation opening with:

> I can report to the American people and to the world that the United States has conducted an operation that killed Osama bin Laden, the leader of Al-Qaeda, and a terrorist who was responsible for the murder of thousands of innocent men, women, and children.

(Author's note: I had two bets: first, that Saddam would be caught alive because he was no religious zealot; and second, that bin Laden, as an extremist, would never allow himself to be captured alive. I won both bets.)

100. THE 2016 ELECTION MAKES HISTORY

While every election is unique, some are more remarkable than others. In the modern digital world, with twenty-four-hour rolling news, minor events can be magnified out of all proportion. An example in the 2016 campaign was Donald Trump who, with his outrageous comments, dominated election news coverage. Trump understood the concept that 'all publicity is good publicity' and turned it into performance art (his great-grandfather turned the German surname Drumpf into Trump). What was truly unique in this recent presidential campaign was that never before in American history has a clear front runner for the nomination not been his political party's preferred candidate.

The Republican Party leaders recognised that a rich, white, bigoted blowhard wouldn't unite the country, and some in the party toyed with the idea of a third candidate. But history has shown, again and again, that America is fundamentally a two-party system, and Trump so successfully manoeuvred himself into pole position that the Republicans had no choice but to choose him to run against Hillary Clinton.

However let's for a moment explore a scenario where Trump becomes the forty-fifth president, in which case it can easily be argued that he'll run into the same problems as Obama. An outsider to Capitol Hill, he is a divisive rather than a unifying figure. The Democrats (and probably some Republicans) will do their utmost to ensure that Trump does not succeed. A Trump presidency will be another failure of political gridlock.

Trump and Obama both appealed to the disenfranchised, only two very different types of disenfranchised voters. Putting it simply, Trump's expressed views appeal mainly to low income, working-class white (usually older) males, and there simply aren't enough of those in America to win a majority. In order to make headlines, Trump has said poisonous things about women, Mexicans, Muslims and other groups who would never consider voting for him. While Trump is a buffoon, he's a shrewd buffoon who has managed to get millions of dollars' worth of free air time both on television and in the social media. His dominance of the media has put him front of mind, but he's front of mind for all the wrong reasons.

In the 2000 election, Hillary Clinton was blindsided by the phenomenon that was Barack Obama, but she has waited patiently for her turn (while serving as Obama's Secretary of State during his first term and using the remaining years to lay the groundwork for the next election). 2016 was her last roll of the dice. A far more accomplished politician than Donald Trump, she was willing to get just as dirty as Trump to win. At the time of writing, this author believes that the 2016 US presidential election will see America with its first woman president ... which also means that Bill and Hillary Clinton are the first presidents to have slept together.